The Data Product Playbook

Designing and Delivering
Data Products that Power
Decisions, Analytics, and AI

Willem Koenders

Technics Publications
SEDONA, ARIZONA

TECHNICS PUBLICATIONS

115 Linda Vista, Sedona, AZ 86336 USA
https://www.TechnicsPub.com

Edited by Steve Hoberman
Cover design by Lorena Molinari

First Printing 2026

ISBN, print ed.	9798898160647
ISBN, Kindle ed.	9798898160654
ISBN, PDF ed.	9798898160661

Contents

Figures

Tables

Acknowledgments

Many people have shaped the way I think about data. The perspectives in this book come from years of learning and being challenged by others. Let me thank a few of them.

I owe a great deal to Carlos Labanda for the years we spent together building and growing Deloitte's data engineering practice across Latin America. Those were among the most formative (and fun!) professional years of my life. Carlos helped sharpen my understanding of analytics in real-world settings, how to design data-driven operating models, how to solve messy problems with structure, and how to keep improving through the right kind of challenge. He is also one of the kindest and most patient people I have ever worked with.

I am deeply grateful to Shri Salem and Florent Moise, both of whom have played defining leadership roles in shaping the data strategy practice at ZS Associates. Their guidance has been foundational to my own development. From Shri, I learned the discipline of identifying the right use cases and quantifying impact with rigor. From Florent, I learned the power of clear communication, crisp narratives, and the importance of connecting ideas into a coherent, compelling arc. Together, they sharpened how I work with clients, giving me the space, time, and intellectual freedom to explore ideas, frameworks, and creativity beyond project work. Their influence sits behind much of the thinking that ultimately shaped this book.

My gratitude extends to Jacklyn Osborne, a senior leader in global banking who quite literally taught me data governance from the ground up. When I first began working with her, I knew practically nothing about the topic. She guided me through the fundamentals by working directly on real problems, from interpreting what data governance actually means, to defining metadata for the first time, to writing my first data quality rules, and to running data councils effectively. Those early hands-on experiences, learned side by side with her, shaped the foundation of everything I now understand about governance and why it matters.

I also thank Molly Chowdhury, whose experience as a technology leader helped me better understand cloud-native approaches to data management and data governance, as well as the cultural factors needed to make them work in real organizations. She also helped me see how to bridge the divide between technology and business teams in a very practical way, showing how to achieve alignment, mobilize cross-functional projects, and create real momentum behind data initiatives.

Working with Kaitlyn Donovan at one of the world's leading medical technology companies has been deeply impactful for me. She is an exceptionally thoughtful leader who plays a key role across both data governance and technology, while also leading real data product teams. Seeing her work up close gave me some of my first firsthand examples of what strong data product practices look like inside a complex technology organization. Several examples in this book are inspired by the kind of thoughtful, user-centered work I saw in her environment.

I am also grateful for my time at Deloitte and for leaders like Tim O'Connor, Nick Cowell, Killian Norvell, Chris Vialle, and Shailender Sidhu, who helped sharpen my thinking. They taught me how to speak clearly with executives, connect analysis to real business decisions, and deliver work that is practical, precise, and useful to the client.

I also want to express my gratitude to Steve Hoberman, whose work in the data management community has influenced countless practitioners, including myself. As the editor and publisher of this book, he allowed me to bring these ideas to life. He guided me through the publishing process with insight, encouragement, and an unfailing commitment to clarity. Working with him has been a fantastic experience. His expertise, patience, and thoughtful feedback strengthened the book in ways that I could not have achieved alone, and I am deeply thankful for the chance to collaborate with him.

Finally, my deepest thanks go to Yuliana Zapata and Charlotte Koenders, my wife and daughter. They are the source of any positive energy I bring into my work and the constant reminder of what truly matters. Their love, patience, and presence have carried me through long nights, demanding projects, and every moment of doubt. They are the loves of my life, and nothing I create would be possible without them.

These people, along with many others whose names could fill pages, helped shape the thinking behind this book. Any clarity or practical value you find here comes from the lessons they taught me along the way.

Introduction

Eighteen months and several million dollars later, a grand data project was ready to launch. It had everything the tech world hypes: a cutting-edge data platform, pipelines ingesting more data than anyone knew what to do with, and a sleek analytics dashboard. It was unveiled with pride, expecting a short-term impact. In the weeks after go-live, however, a troubling fact emerged: hardly anyone was using it.

This wasn't the first time I'd seen a promising data initiative fall flat. In retrospect, the team had been so focused on technology and data for their own sake that it had lost sight of the people who were supposed to use them.

A classic case of "build it and they will come" – and then they didn't.

Roughly at the same time, at a different organization, I witnessed something that seemed like the opposite scenario. A small team cobbled together a simple database and put it on a SharePoint location to meet an urgent business need. There was nothing fancy about it: no AI algorithms, no big budget – just a clear focus on a pressing question and a willingness to iterate with feedback. The dataset quickly went viral internally. Within a month, employees across departments were using it daily. That simple database, built in weeks, had a visible impact on decisions and boosted the bottom line of this global company.

The contrast between these two cases stood out to me. Why did one fail so spectacularly, despite resources and talent, while the other succeeded on a shoestring? The answer, I came to realize, lies in how we define and deliver data. Data only becomes an asset when it is shaped with intention, designed for usability, and stewarded with care. That's the promise of the data product approach. It treats data as something purposeful, discoverable, and reusable, created with the same discipline as a product, with a user in mind. The best example of treating data as an asset is to consider data products.

Indeed, in many boardrooms around the world, it's now commonplace to hear that "data is our greatest asset." I've seen this belief firsthand in my work, coauthoring more than 100 data strategies with data leaders across Europe, Asia, North America, Latin America, and Africa, spanning industries from banking and insurance to manufacturing, medical technology, healthcare, and the public sector. Despite heavy investments in data initiatives, many organizations struggle to realize value. Studies keep showing that most analytics projects fail to deliver the expected business outcomes because the underlying data is not ready. And now, with the surge of AI, and specifically generative and agentic AI, this weakness is even harder to ignore.

These new tools create huge excitement, but they also make the same truth obvious again: nothing works without good, ready-to-use data.

The models are not the real bottleneck. The data is. Organizations are learning that if they want AI to scale and deliver real value, they need data that is well designed, trusted, easy to find, and consistent across the business. In other words, they need data products.

This book will show how to put a data product approach into practice. Chapter 1 covers the foundational concepts of data products and why they matter. Chapter 2 dives into technical and design implementation, and how to build data products with the right tools and processes. Chapter 3 focuses on people and change management, exploring how to drive adoption and embed these solutions into the organizational culture. Throughout, you'll see real-world examples and insights drawn from my global experience. The goal is to equip you to treat data as an asset by developing data products that people embrace and deliver lasting business results.

Chapter 1

Data Product Foundations

This chapter answers a simple but important question: What do we actually mean when we say "data product," and how can you identify one when you see it? Many teams use the term for almost anything with data in it. In this chapter, we provide a clear working definition and show what makes a real data product different from a loose table or a one-off report.

First, we introduce the idea of a data product as a reusable, governed, user-oriented data asset. We then break this idea down into clear properties, which are the traits that every true data product should have. Finally, we walk through the main types of data products you are likely to see in practice, grouping them into source-oriented and use-oriented products, and providing practical examples.

1.1. What is a Data Product?

Walk into any enterprise today, and you'll hear the term *data product* floating around. Sometimes it refers to a dashboard, other times a dataset, or maybe a table in the data warehouse. The label is everywhere, but the meaning isn't always clear.

At its core, a data product is a well-defined, reusable, governed, and user-oriented data asset.

It is designed to serve a specific purpose, be accessible and understandable to its intended users, and be reliable enough to support repeated, high-value use. It might take various forms and sizes, but what sets it apart from ad hoc data artifacts is the intentional structure and service mindset behind it.

A data product is not just "data"; it's data delivered as a product, with clear ownership, consistent standards, and ongoing stewardship.

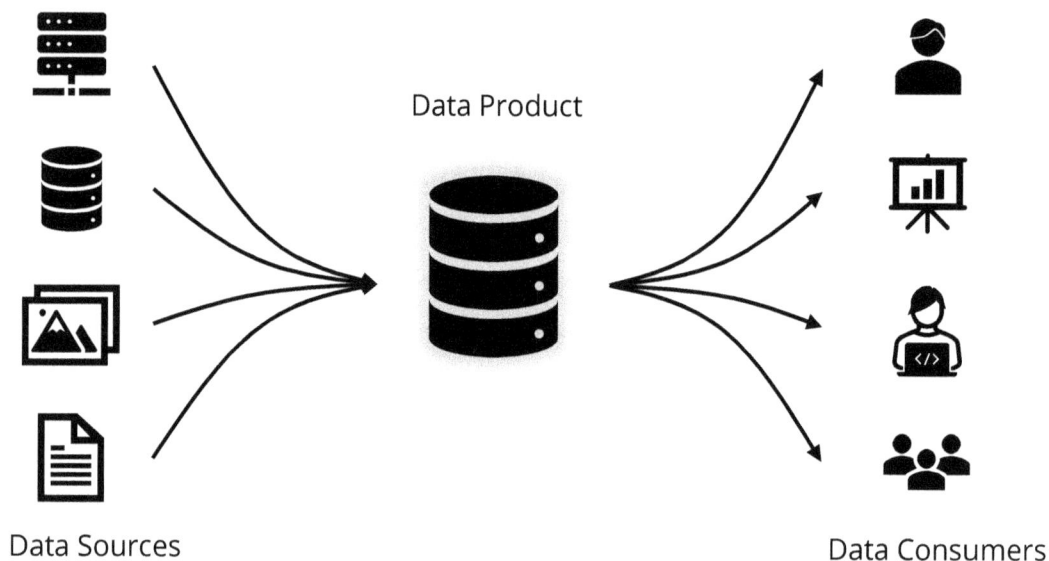

Figure 1 – A simple schematic of a data product.

To bring the concept to life, take a look at Figure 1, perhaps the simplest possible depiction of what a data product looks like in practice. On the left, we see data sources. There might be a single source or hundreds of feeds converging into a single product. Source data might be structured, coming from enterprise systems like ERP or CRM databases, or unstructured formats like documents or images. At the center is the data product itself, which is the curated and usable asset shaped from these raw inputs. On the right are the data consumers. These might be business teams, individual analysts, software developers, or even automated systems and workflows. The key is that consumption is purposeful and valuable. What you don't see in this image but what is essential, are the supporting infrastructure components, such as data platforms, pipelines, storage, cleansing capabilities, AI enrichment, and more. We'll explore them in greater detail in the coming sections.

Let's consider an analogy. Imagine a busy, high-pressure kitchen in a top-tier restaurant. The chefs aren't out in the fields growing carrots or milling their own flour. They rely on high-quality ingredients to be prepared, labeled, and ready to use. Their focus is on creating something valuable for their customers. A dish that's timely, unique, and composed with care.

But what happens if the salt looks like sugar? If the chicken is unlabeled? If the tomatoes are missing entirely? Suddenly, those chefs can't do their job. Their creativity, speed, and precision break down. Instead of focusing on the meal, they're now scrambling just to identify what's in front of them. Worse, each chef might start stockpiling their own ingredients, creating waste, duplication, and chaos.

What great chefs want is to work with clean, clearly labeled, reliable ingredients that they can combine in just the right way, at the right time, for the specific people they're serving. And ideally, they want shared access, so every station doesn't need its own secret stash of onions or butter. They don't want to worry about basic ingredients; they want to focus on creating that spectacular new dish.

This is similar to the situation in many organizations when it comes to data. Analysts, data scientists, and business users don't want to spend their time stitching together incomplete tables or emailing three teams to find the "real" source of truth. Like chefs, their job should be to combine and apply data. But too often, the raw ingredients are poorly labeled, inconsistently formatted, or scattered across silos.

This is where data products come in. Just like well-prepped ingredients in a professional kitchen, data products are clearly defined, reliable, available in a known location, and ready to use. They're intentionally designed to be accessed by many "chefs" across the business, each of whom might use them differently, but all of whom can trust that they're using the same, high-quality component. The power of data products lies in this composability and trust. They are data assets usable out of the box, again and again, by different teams across different contexts, without confusion or unnecessary rework.

1.2. Key Properties of Data Products

To build and manage effective data products, it helps to be clear about what defines them. That starts with their properties. These are the core traits that make a data product distinct from a generic dataset or dashboard. A property is not just a desirable feature; it's a defining characteristic that signals the product is usable, trusted, and reusable across different teams and tools. These properties also work in reverse: if something exhibits them, it can rightfully be considered a true data product.

By making these properties explicit, organizations create a shared understanding of what good looks like, which helps ensure consistency, foster accountability, and build trust with both creators and consumers. These properties can also inform certification criteria (see Section 2.3.4. Certification of Data Products) and maturity measures (see Section 3.3.1. Maturity Framework for Individual Data Products). Figure 2 outlines these key properties.

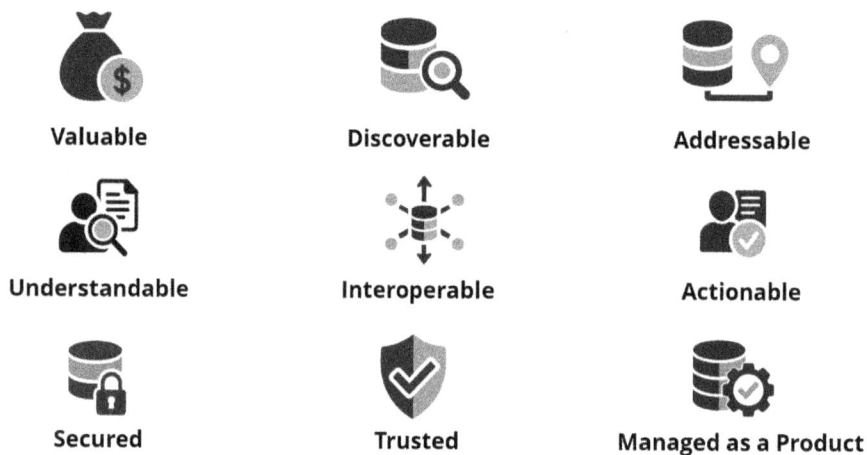

Valuable **Discoverable** **Addressable**

Understandable **Interoperable** **Actionable**

Secured **Trusted** **Managed as a Product**

Figure 2 – The nine defining properties of data products.

1. **Valuable:** A data product must deliver clear, tangible value. That value usually ties to explicitly defined business use cases, through which revenue may be increased, costs reduced, customer and employee experience enhanced, or risk mitigated. The value should not be vague or assumed; it should be clearly articulated, ideally quantified, and traceable back to its impact. A data product without a measurable or observable use is not a data product. And this isn't a one-time exercise. Value should be reviewed over time to ensure the product continues to serve a relevant purpose as business needs evolve.

2. **Discoverable:** A data product must be easy to find by both business and technical users. That usually means it is registered in a data catalog, included in dashboards or wikis, and named using consistent conventions. There are opportunities to actively create awareness, such as internal showcases, documentation, and curated collections, so users know what is available, what it is for, and when to use it. Discoverability enables self-service, cross-functional reuse, and faster time-to-insight.

3. **Addressable:** A data product has a known, stable, and consistent location, such as a persistent table path, API endpoint, or web URL. The concept ensures that users or systems can reliably point to the product and integrate it into workflows without fear of sudden change or disappearance. It is about ensuring continuity. Just like a chef expects tomatoes to be in the same fridge every day, data consumers need their critical inputs to be dependable and consistently located.

4. **Understandable:** A data product must be unambiguous and easy to interpret. When a user finds it, they should be able to grasp what the product contains, how it is structured, and how it should or should not be used. This is usually enabled through business and technical metadata, including field definitions, applied business rules, limitations, and usage guidance. Often, this content lives in a combination of a business glossary, data dictionary, and data catalog.

5. **Interoperable:** A data product is interoperable when it can be easily used across the tools, systems, and workflows that consumers already rely on. Closely related concepts include accessibility, ensuring authorized users can reliably reach the product, and composability, allowing it to be combined with other data products or embedded into downstream systems. This means that the data works smoothly with standard interfaces such as SQL, APIs, dashboards, notebooks, or automated pipelines without custom adapters or complicated workarounds.

6. **Actionable:** A data product is actionable when it can be used directly to support decisions or actions without requiring significant additional work. Once a user has access, they should not need to repeatedly clean the data, reconcile sources, adjust definitions, or perform manual preparation before it becomes useful. The data is already curated and

aligned to its intended use cases, reducing friction between access and impact and allowing teams to move quickly from data to informed action.

7. **Secured:** A data product must be protected according to the sensitivity and classification of its contents. That includes implementing access controls, enforcing data masking or anonymization, logging access, and ensuring proper entitlements. Only the right people, for the right purposes, should be able to use the data. Without appropriate safeguards, the data product risks violating compliance, privacy, or ethical standards, and it cannot be trusted or scaled.

8. **Trusted:** Users know what to expect. The product is accurate, complete, timely, and reliable. This typically requires automated quality checks, freshness indicators, and validation against defined standards. Version control and change logging may also be key and are often embedded into the trustworthiness of the product. Users should never be surprised by shifts in logic or content. A trusted product signals that it is ready for business-critical use and that its producers stand behind its quality.

9. **Managed as a Product:** Every data product must have a clear owner and support model. Ownership is not just about creating the product. It is about evolving it. It should be managed through a backlog, a roadmap, and continuous consumer input. That means tracking feedback, updating features, deprecating outdated logic, and ensuring the product continues to meet current and future needs. Consumer needs may shift next year or next quarter, and the product should adapt. Like any other product, its long-term value depends on active listening and intentional iteration.

To make these nine properties even more tangible, let's apply them to our simple kitchen analogy. Imagine a container of prepared tomatoes. By walking through each property in that context, we can see how these traits come to life in a familiar, real-world setting:

1. **Valuable:** The tomatoes save time and add consistency. They're used in real dishes that customers order, which means they clearly serve a purpose and create value.

2. **Discoverable:** The tomatoes appear on the daily mise en place list, visible to everyone. Chefs scanning the list can quickly discover that prepped tomatoes are available without digging through the fridge.

3. **Addressable:** They always live in the same spot: second shelf of the fridge, on the left side. The chef doesn't have to guess where they are or worry they've been moved randomly.

4. **Understandable:** The container is clearly labeled, e.g., "Chopped San Marzano Tomatoes – Cooked – No Salt." Everyone in the kitchen knows what's inside and how to use it.

5. **Interoperable:** Any chef with permission can open the fridge, take the tomatoes, and use them in their process, whether in a pot, a blender, or a saucepan.

6. **Actionable:** The tomatoes are ready to use the moment a chef needs them. There is no extra washing, cutting, seasoning, or quality checking required before they can be added to a dish.

7. **Secured:** The container is sealed, stored properly, and only accessible to kitchen staff. It's not left out to spoil or be tampered with.

8. **Trusted:** The tomatoes are checked for freshness and quality when stored. Chefs trust the ingredient because it's consistent, has a reliable taste, and there are clear agreements with the supplier to ensure quality and availability.

9. **Managed as a Product:** A specific person in the kitchen is responsible for prepping, labeling, and maintaining the tomato container. If chefs give feedback (e.g., "cut them finer" or "we need more on Tuesdays"), changes are made.

1.3. Types and Examples of Data Products

There are many different kinds of data products. In this section, we'll unpack what typically falls under this definition of a data product and what types of data products exist.

Some of the confusion starts with the distinction (or lack thereof) between data products and data assets. In common usage, *a data asset refers* to any data entity that has some form of value—anything from a raw dataset to a report or a full dashboard. Data products, on the other hand, are usually defined with greater intention. It's data that has been designed and managed with a user in mind:

with clear value, ownership, documentation, access, and reusability baked in, as we discussed in Sections 1.1 and 1.2 already.

Every data product is a data asset, but not every data asset qualifies as a data product.

That said, in most conversations with client organizations and my own teams, I'm comfortable using the terms relatively interchangeably. While there may be nuance in certain enterprise or academic contexts, in most of the real-world work I've done, the distinction isn't particularly helpful or necessary. For this book, I'll use data product as the preferred term.

Now, if we want to make sense of the variety of data products out there, it helps to group them in ways that reflect how they're actually built, used, and managed. One framework that's worked well in practice is to distinguish between two main types: Source-Oriented Data Products and Use-Oriented Data Products.

Source-Oriented Data Products are those that tend to resemble the structure and purpose of core enterprise platforms and processes.

They are typically derived from systems such as ERP, CRM, finance platforms, or other operational tools where business-critical data is originally created or recorded. These data products do not radically transform the data. Instead, they curate or lightly refine it, often resolving quality issues or ensuring consistency, so that it can be more broadly useful beyond the source system. For example, while the sales module in an ERP system may generate transactional records for its own internal use, a source-oriented data product might extract and organize that same data to make it available for analytics, reporting, or integration with other systems. These products are usually stable, standardized, and designed for reuse across many different teams and processes without altering their fundamental structure or meaning.

Use-Oriented Data Products are created closer to the point of consumption and decision-making.

Rather than reflecting the structure of a foundational system, they are shaped around the needs of specific use cases or business consumers. These data products often integrate multiple upstream sources, and the data within them is transformed, aggregated, enriched, or modeled to support a particular objective. The focus is on actionability, packaging the data in exactly the right shape, granularity, or context to enable a dashboard, power a machine learning model, or inform a workflow. The lineage from raw source data may be harder to trace directly, but the product itself is tightly aligned to business outcomes. In many cases, use-oriented data products build on source-oriented ones, combining and reshaping them to deliver immediate insights or support specific tools and applications.

In Table 1 below, we list the six most common data product types across these two categories, along with example data products for each.

Category	Type	Examples
Source-Oriented	Reference Data Products	Country codes, product taxonomies, currency tables
	Mastered Data Products	Customer 360, Provider Master, Product Master
	Transactional Data Products	Orders, claims, clicks, invoice line items
Use-Oriented	Analytical Data Products	Sales dashboards, daily user counts, quarterly forecasts
	Model-Driven Data Products	Churn scores, next-best-offers, fraud risk ratings
	Experience-Oriented Data Products	BI dashboards, real-time alerts, embedded data visualizations

Table 1 – Subtypes of Data Products.

Let's unpack each of these data product types further.

Source-Oriented Data Products Type 1: Reference Data Products

Reference data products capture small, finite sets of standardized values that are used across many systems to ensure consistency and clarity. By definition, these are bounded lists. There is a defined, limited set of valid entries that rarely change. A classic example is country codes or country names. There are only so many countries in the world, and having a single, centrally managed table ensures that every system and team uses the same way of referring to "Germany" or "DE." Other examples include currency codes, units of measure, product categories, or medical procedure classifications.

These tables are critical for validation, mapping, reporting, and categorization across enterprise systems. While they may seem simple, their consistency and correctness have wide-reaching impacts. Because they don't change often and are shared across domains, reference data products are ideal candidates for central governance and distribution.

Refer to Table 2 below for an example of a reference data product containing standardized country codes.

Country Name	ISO Alpha-2 Code	ISO Alpha-3 Code	Numeric Code	Region
United States	US	USA	840	Americas
Germany	DE	DEU	276	Europe
Brazil	BR	BRA	076	Americas
Japan	JP	JPN	392	Asia
South Africa	ZA	ZAF	710	Africa

Table 2 – Reference Data Product of Country Codes.

Source-Oriented Data Products Type 2: Master Data Products

Master data products manage the core business entities that a company interacts with—customers, products, suppliers, employees, locations, and more. Unlike reference data, master data isn't inherently bounded. New records can be added or removed frequently as new clients are acquired, new products launched, or employees hired or terminated. Still, what master data shares with reference data is the intent to create a single, unique list per domain: a single version of the truth that describes each entity in a clear, complete, and standardized way. The challenge with master data lies in harmonization—bringing together information from multiple systems, resolving duplicates, standardizing formats, and reconciling business rules. For example, a Customer Master data product might pull data from CRM systems, marketing platforms, and order management systems to build a unified view of each customer. These data products can be critical for analytics, seamless operations, personalization, compliance, and reporting across the organization.

Refer to Table 3 below for an example of a master data product containing core customer records.

Customer ID	Full Name	Date of Birth	Country	Customer Segment	Status
CUST001	Maria Gutierrez	1985-07-12	US	Retail	Active
CUST002	Ahmed El-Sayed	1978-11-03	EG	Enterprise	Inactive
CUST003	Jun Nakamura	1990-02-27	JP	SME	Active
CUST004	Fatima Mbaye	1983-09-15	SN	Retail	Active
CUST005	John Müller	1969-05-19	DE	Enterprise	Suspended

Table 3 – Sample part of a Customer Master data product.

Source-Oriented Data Products Type 3: Transactional Data Products

Transactional data products capture the activities that occur in the business every day. This can include actual financial transactions, such as purchases, refunds, or claims, but it's not limited to them. The term "transactional" here refers more broadly to records of discrete, repeated business events or process steps. This includes sales orders, shipments, invoices, call center interactions, audit logs, and even internal actions such as onboarding steps or system status updates. While these records are typically stored in source systems in operational formats, transactional data products curate them into cleaner, well-structured formats optimized for reuse. They maintain the integrity of the original events while ensuring they are queryable, consistently timestamped, and reliably joinable with other products such as master data. These data products are critical inputs for metrics, models, and dashboards across the enterprise and are among the most reused assets in any analytics ecosystem. Table 4 shows a transactional data product capturing customer purchase events.

Transaction ID	Customer ID	Transaction Date	Product ID	Quantity	Total Amount	Payment Method	Channel
TXN1001	CUST001	2025-06-01	PROD234	2	49.98	Credit Card	In-Store
TXN1002	CUST003	2025-06-02	PROD119	1	15.99	PayPal	Online
TXN1003	CUST004	2025-06-03	PROD234	3	74.97	Credit Card	Online
TXN1004	CUST001	2025-06-03	PROD098	1	22.00	Gift Card	In-Store
TXN1005	CUST005	2025-06-04	PROD300	5	125.00	Bank Transfer	B2B Portal

Table 4 – Purchase Transactions Log.

Use-Oriented Data Product Type 1: Analytical Data Products

Analytical data products are built by transforming and enriching foundational datasets, which are core datasets that form the organization's shared data backbone. These foundational datasets are often the source data products discussed earlier, such as reference data, mastered data, and transactional records. These products are usually designed to serve specific analytical purposes, and to support insight generation and decision-making. They go beyond raw or curated source data by applying calculations, aggregations, business logic, and, sometimes, data enrichment from third-party sources. The result is a dataset immediately usable by analysts, business leaders, or data scientists, tailored to a specific domain or objective (e.g., sales performance, customer retention, supply chain efficiency). Analytical data products are often refreshed on a regular cadence and version-controlled to ensure consistency over time. Refer to Table 5 below for an example of an analytical data product that summarizes monthly customer spend and behavior metrics.

Customer ID	Month	Total Spend	Avg Order Value	Orders Count	Last Purchase Date	Loyalty Tier	Active Campaign Target
CUST001	2025-05	189.94	47.49	4	2025-05-28	Gold	Yes
CUST002	2025-05	32.00	32.00	1	2025-05-10	Silver	No
CUST003	2025-05	108.75	36.25	3	2025-05-22	Bronze	Yes
CUST004	2025-05	225.00	75.00	3	2025-05-30	Gold	No
CUST005	2025-05	58.99	58.99	1	2025-05-16	Silver	Yes

Table 5 – Monthly Customer Spend and Engagement Summary.

Use-Oriented Data Product Type 2: Model-Driven Data Products

Model-driven data products are the outputs of machine learning, AI, or statistical models that have been turned into reusable, consumable assets. These are often predictive or scoring datasets that feed into decision engines, marketing campaigns, risk systems, or customer experiences. They typically depend on rich source data, structured feature engineering, and ongoing model governance. These data products are often refreshed on a recurring basis (daily, weekly, monthly) and are accompanied by metadata about model version, confidence levels, and context in which the predictions should or shouldn't be used. See Table 6 for a model-driven data product predicting customer churn risk.

Customer ID	Prediction Date	Churn Risk Score	Risk Tier	Model Version	Next Best Action
CUST001	2025-06-01	0.87	High	v2.3	Offer retention deal
CUST002	2025-06-01	0.12	Low	v2.3	No action needed
CUST003	2025-06-01	0.45	Medium	v2.3	Send re-engagement email
CUST004	2025-06-01	0.72	High	v2.3	Call from agent
CUST005	2025-06-01	0.29	Low	v2.3	Monitor activity

Table 6 – Data product with customer churn risk scores and associated next best actions.

Use-Oriented Data Product Type 3: Experience-Oriented Data Products

Experience-oriented data products are those that include not just the data itself, but also the user interface or presentation layer through which the data is accessed and consumed. These often take the form of dashboards, self-service tools, real-time alerts, or embedded analytics views. What makes them data products is not just the visual component, but the fact that the underlying data has been packaged with a clear purpose. These products aim to provide actionable insights at the point of need, often to a business user or operational role. They typically combine data from multiple other products, apply business rules, and are designed for decision-making.

For a concrete illustration, Table 7 shows an example of a structured data feed that could power the UI layer of such a data product, while Figure 3 provides a visual example of what an experience-oriented sales dashboard might look like in practice.

Region	Week Ending	Total Sales	Target Sales	Performance Status	Last Refreshed
North	2025-06-01	$2,340,000	$2,500,000	Below Target	2025-06-02 07:15 AM
South	2025-06-01	$2,680,000	$2,600,000	Exceeding Target	2025-06-02 07:15 AM
East	2025-06-01	$1,980,000	$2,100,000	Slightly Below	2025-06-02 07:15 AM
West	2025-06-01	$2,700,000	$2,700,000	On Target	2025-06-02 07:15 AM

Table 7 – Example of a regional sales performance dashboard feed.

Figure 3 – Example of a sales dashboard. Source (Geckoboard, 2025).

The Six Types of Data Products in Context

Together, these six types form a mutually exclusive and collectively exhaustive framework. That is to say, any data product you ever come across will fit into at least one of these categories. Depending on how it's built, a product might touch on more than one category, but in practice, virtually all data products fit predominantly into one of these six. In my own work with clients across industries, we've nearly always focused on the first four: reference, master, transactional, and analytical data products. These are the ones most consistently reused, most foundational in architecture, and most aligned with the mindset of reusable, governed, and intentional design. That's not to dismiss model-driven or experience-oriented data products; they are absolutely valid, often powerful, and in some organizations play a central role in delivering value. But they are typically more tightly bound to a specific use case, interface, or workflow, and thus, much less reusable in the broader sense. For that reason, they've often fallen outside my core working definition of a data product, because for me, a true data product is one where the data itself is the centerpiece of what's being delivered.

This structure—source-oriented versus use-oriented, with six subtypes—isn't the only way to slice the space, but it's a model helpful across a wide variety of teams and organizational contexts. It gives us a common language to classify data products, understand how they're built and consumed, and prioritize where to focus our efforts. When I talk about data products, I'll be referring to those types where data itself is the primary unit of value, particularly the foundational source-oriented categories and the analytical layer that builds directly upon them.

CHAPTER 2

Designing and Building Great Data Products

In Chapter 1, we focused on what data products are and why they matter. In this part of the book, we shift from concept to execution: how to actually design, build, and run data products in a way that is intentional, repeatable, and tied to business value.

We'll start by introducing a **data product lifecycle** that breaks the journey into eight practical phases, from planning and analysis through design, build, deployment, usage, maintenance, and eventual retirement. This lifecycle provides teams with a common language for their work, clarifies handoffs between roles, and reduces the risk of skipping important steps. Throughout the chapter, we'll keep coming back to this lifecycle as the backbone of how strong data products are created and managed over time.

Once the lifecycle is in place, we turn to **value quantification and the business case**. A data product is only worth building if it clearly contributes to outcomes like revenue uplift, cost reduction, better experiences, or risk mitigation. We'll walk through a simple, reusable business case template and apply it to a concrete example: the Finance Reconciliation Engine. You'll see how to connect specific use cases to value levers, estimate benefits and costs, and translate them into ROI and payback periods that can stand up to finance and senior leadership.

Finally, we zoom in on **data product blueprints and architectural guidelines**. Even the best lifecycle and business case won't help if every team invents its own one-off solution. To avoid that, we'll define a reference data architecture and a set of architectural standards that teams can use as a starting point. We'll show how to realize this architecture on platforms like AWS and how a small number of product, coding, metadata, quality, and access guidelines can dramatically improve consistency, reusability, and governance across your portfolio.

Taken together, these three elements—the end-to-end lifecycle, business case, and architectural blueprints—form the core of executing data products well. By the end of this part, you should have a clear, practical toolkit not just for talking about data products, but for planning, justifying, and building them in a way that scales.

2.1. Data Product Lifecycle

To truly deliver value, data products require intentional execution across their full lifecycle. This section introduces a practical framework for describing and managing that end-to-end journey.

The data product lifecycle is a structured view of how data products are planned, built, deployed, and maintained over time. It breaks the work into eight key phases, from initial ideation to eventual retirement, and outlines the typical activities that take place in each. It gives teams a common language, clarifies ownership handoffs, and ensures that nothing critical is missed along the way. You can see an overview in Figure 4, which lays out the eight phases involved in bringing a data product to life, and keeping it healthy.

In the rest of this section, we'll walk through each of the eight phases at a high level. Later in the book, we'll return to specific moments within this lifecycle to double-click on topics like value quantification, roles and responsibilities, certification, governance, and product iteration.

2.1.1. Planning

The planning phase marks the starting point of any data product journey. It's where early ideas take shape and begin to translate into concrete plans. This stage is about moving from loose ambition to structured intent, clarifying what the data product should be, why it matters, and how it will be resourced and executed. It sets the foundation for everything that follows.

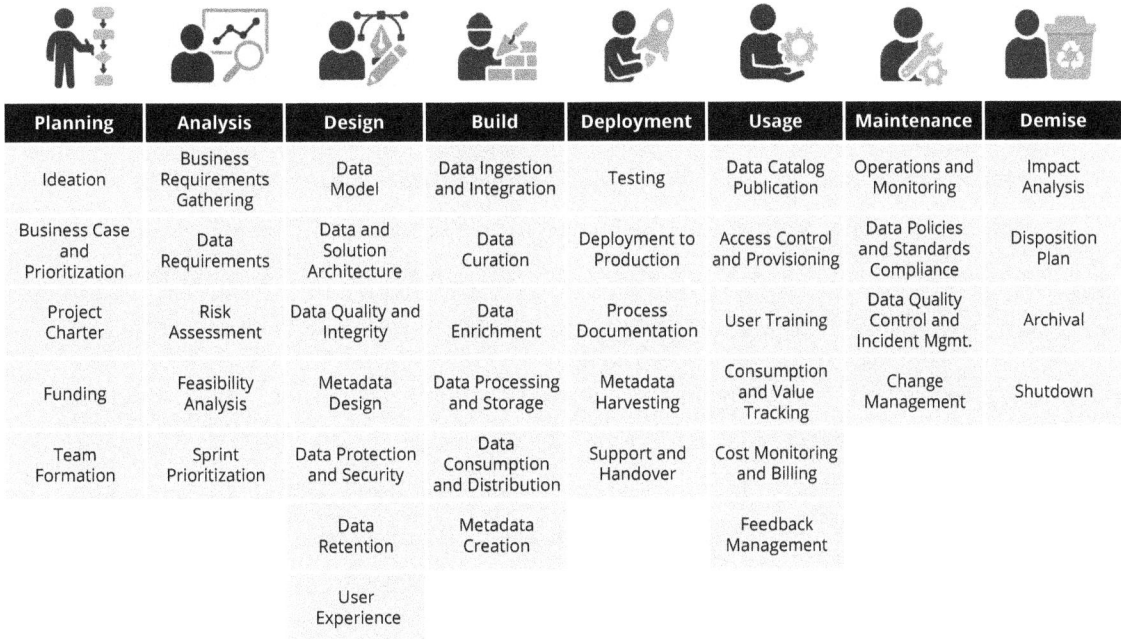

Planning	Analysis	Design	Build	Deployment	Usage	Maintenance	Demise
Ideation	Business Requirements Gathering	Data Model	Data Ingestion and Integration	Testing	Data Catalog Publication	Operations and Monitoring	Impact Analysis
Business Case and Prioritization	Data Requirements	Data and Solution Architecture	Data Curation	Deployment to Production	Access Control and Provisioning	Data Policies and Standards Compliance	Disposition Plan
Project Charter	Risk Assessment	Data Quality and Integrity	Data Enrichment	Process Documentation	User Training	Data Quality Control and Incident Mgmt.	Archival
Funding	Feasibility Analysis	Metadata Design	Data Processing and Storage	Metadata Harvesting	Consumption and Value Tracking	Change Management	Shutdown
Team Formation	Sprint Prioritization	Data Protection and Security	Data Consumption and Distribution	Support and Handover	Cost Monitoring and Billing		
		Data Retention	Metadata Creation		Feedback Management		
		User Experience					

Figure 4 – End-to-end data product lifecycle.

Good planning is critical because it ensures that the effort to build a data product is purposeful and aligned with organizational priorities. Without clear planning, teams risk wasting time on low-impact work, duplicating efforts, or building something that lacks support or viability. Getting stakeholder alignment early reduces churn later. By clarifying the "why," "what," and "how," this phase de-risks the entire lifecycle.

- **Ideation:** The process of generating and capturing new ideas for data products. Sometimes these ideas emerge organically, sparked by a clear business problem or internal pain point. Beyond spontaneous suggestions, organizations can benefit greatly from encouraging a broader mindset that treats data as an asset and explores how to productionize it. When teams across functions understand the possibilities of data products and see relevant examples, they are much more likely to surface meaningful ideas and opportunities that can be refined and prioritized.

- **Business Case and Prioritization:** Once ideas are captured, they need to be evaluated for impact, effort, and alignment. This step typically involves building a lightweight business case to articulate the expected benefits, such as increased revenue, cost savings, or reduced risk. One of the most effective ways to do this is to anchor the proposed data product in known business processes or use cases, as we will see in more detail in Section 2.2. Value Quantification and Business Case. Having an enterprise inventory of high-priority business processes and their owners, along with defined value statements, makes it significantly easier to make the case for specific data products. As we will outline later, a structured approach to mapping and quantifying value is essential for prioritization and portfolio management (see 3.2. Building a Portfolio of Data Products).

- **Project Charter:** A short, written document that aligns all stakeholders on the scope, objectives, success criteria, and key roles. A Project Charter might sound overly formal, but it doesn't have to be. In my experience, most teams don't go through the effort of drafting one, but I think they should. With today's language models, you can get a template and draft a solid project charter in minutes. Doing so dramatically improves clarity and accelerates decision-making later in the lifecycle. This project charter serves as the foundation for more detailed planning and coordination, and you can always go back to it and update it based on new insights and feedback. In Figure 5, you can find a simple example of such a project charter. Here, for the first time, we introduce the "Finance Reconciliation Engine" data product, which we'll continue to use throughout this book and which will be introduced in more detail in subsequent sections.

- **Funding:** With a defined scope and clear value, the next step is securing the necessary resources. This may involve tapping into centralized budget pools, seeking department-level funding, or negotiating allocation from shared delivery teams. Even in agile or lightweight environments, some level of funding clarity is needed before significant effort begins. This step helps ensure the right support is in place to move from planning into execution.

- **Team Formation:** The final step in the planning phase is assembling the right team. There are two layers to consider here. First, identify the core roles that will be critical throughout the lifecycle. This typically includes a data product owner, a data engineer, and someone focused on governance or quality. These individuals should be engaged early and consistently. Then, identify the broader set of contributors who may support specific stages or deliverables, such as UX designers, domain experts, security leads, or DevOps engineers. It helps tremendously to work from a clear role template that outlines typical responsibilities across the full lifecycle. In the next chapter (specifically, 3.1. Data Product Teams, Roles, and Responsibilities), we will walk through these roles and responsibilities in more detail.

Data Product Working Title: *Finance Reconciliation Engine*

High-Level Description	This data product will automatically reconcile financial transactions across ERP systems, bank statements, and payment processor feeds. It reduces manual effort and provides a single, trusted daily view of matched and unmatched transactions.	*Explains what the data product aims to achieve and why it matters*
Key Stakeholders	Data Product Owner – Emily Carter Data Engineering Lead – Ravi Deshmukh Business Sponsor – Laura McKinney (VP Finance Operations) Governance & Quality Lead – Marcus Li Security & Privacy Partner – Sofia Delgado Finance Process SME – Daniel Ortiz	*Lists the main people involved and their role or interest in the data product*
Goals and Success Criteria	✓ Automate core reconciliation steps and reduce manual effort. ✓ Provide one reliable daily dataset of matched and unmatched transactions. ✓ Improve transparency for finance and audit teams.	*What outcomes do we expect? How do we know it worked?*
Timelines and Expectations	❑ Analysis complete by Week 4 ❑ Initial design blueprint by Week 8 ❑ First usable slice (MVP) by Week 18 ❑ Full rollout target by Week 24	*A lightweight view of milestone expectations*
Dependencies, Assumptions, and Risks	• Access to ERP, bank, and processor data must be granted on time. • Finance SMEs and engineering support must be available throughout. • Data quality issues or delayed feeds may slow or limit MVP delivery	*Highlights known risks and key assumptions that could affect delivery*

Figure 5 – An illustrative data product project charter template for the Finance Reconciliation Engine data product.

> *When done well, the planning phase creates clarity and momentum. It ensures the data product is grounded in real need, supported by the right people, and set up to succeed.*

2.1.2. Analysis

The analysis phase is where clarity starts to take shape. After the planning phase has set direction and secured resources, this is the moment to dig deeper and define exactly what is needed and why. It's about translating an initial idea into a structured understanding of the problem space, user needs, risks, and technical realities. A good analysis phase helps ensure that the team builds the right thing in the right way, and that everyone involved shares a common understanding of what success should look like.

This phase is especially important because without it, teams risk building products that are either misaligned with business needs or technically unfeasible. In my experience, some of the most costly missteps in data product development happen when teams skip this step or treat it as a formality.

---

*Rushing into development without a firm grasp of requirements or constraints
often leads to rework or outright failure.*

Business Requirements Gathering

This is the process of engaging stakeholders to understand what the data product needs to do. That means going beyond surface-level asks like "we want a dashboard" or "give us a list of customers" and digging into the decisions they're trying to make, the workflows they follow, and the pain points they encounter today. Good requirement gathering is collaborative and often iterative. It may involve interviews, workshops, or shadowing users to uncover the underlying jobs-to-be-done and the specific features or data elements that will make the product truly useful.

One common output here is a Business Requirements Document (BRD). It captures the key business goals, intended users, success metrics, and high-level functionality expected from the data product. It doesn't have to be overly complex, but having something written down early helps clarify direction and create alignment. A BRD may cover several kinds of requirements depending on the nature of the product, including:

- **Functional requirements**: What the product should do or provide from a business perspective.

- **Non-functional requirements**: Performance, scalability, availability, usability, and other quality attributes.

- **Operational requirements**: How the product will be supported, maintained, and monitored.

Figure 6 below shows some sample requirements as part of a broader BRD.

Business Requirements Document: *Finance Reconciliation Engine*

Functional Requirements	**1.1 Data Ingestion and Connectivity** 1.1.1 The system shall ingest ERP transaction data on a daily basis, with the ability to configure additional intraday refreshes. 1.1.2 The system shall ingest bank statements from all supported banks using secure automated feeds (API or SFTP). 1.1.3 …
Non-Functional Requirements	**2.1 Performance and Scalability** 2.1.1 The system shall process one full day of transactions (up to five million records) within 60 minutes. 2.1.2 The system shall scale to handle peak load events (e.g., month-end spikes) without degradation. 2.1.3 …
Operational Requirements	**3.1 Support and Maintenance** 3.1.1 A Level two support team shall be available during business hours to handle ingestion issues and pipeline errors. 3.1.2 A monthly maintenance window shall be defined for updates, patching, and feature deployments. 3.1.3 …

Figure 6 – Sample BRD for Finance Reconciliation Engine data product.

Data Requirements

Since we are building a data product, being clear about the data that is actually needed is particularly critical. This includes identifying which data elements are required, where they will come from, and what quality, freshness, granularity, and completeness they require. Teams should ask themselves: Do we already have this data? Is it available in the required shape and quality? What gaps exist, and how critical are they?

These questions are not academic. Especially for more advanced data-driven use cases that include (generative) AI, predictive models, or sophisticated analytics, more than 50% of the time is spent just finding, cleaning, and preparing the data. If teams skip over the step of clearly defining their data requirements upfront, they are almost guaranteed to hit major blockers or delays later.

Risk Assessment

Once needs are defined, it's critical to explore what could go wrong. Risk assessment involves identifying technical, operational, legal, or organizational risks that could derail the project. For example, will the data be available at the expected quality or latency? Are there compliance requirements for handling personal or sensitive data? Could integration with a legacy system introduce delays? By flagging risks early, teams can avoid surprises and plan mitigations before problems arise.

This moment is also one of the most important opportunities to bring together legal, privacy, compliance, and related governance teams. Many of the painful retroactive cleanup efforts that follow data breaches, regulatory issues, or internal audits stem from stakeholders not being involved early enough. And usually, they actually really want to be involved. Most privacy and legal teams do not want to show up late to fix broken things. They would much rather help shape things properly from the start. I know many business teams see involving them as a bureaucratic delay, but I would strongly recommend against sidestepping this. It is far more efficient and far less risky to have them engaged now. And if you're part of the privacy or legal team, I would encourage you to be practical. Don't let this turn into a theoretical exercise that tries to rule out every possible future risk. Focus on the key concerns, define reasonable guardrails, and help the team move forward responsibly.

Depending on the maturity of your organization, this is also the right time to conduct a Privacy Impact Assessment (PIA). A PIA is a structured review that identifies potential privacy risks and defines how they will be mitigated. It typically includes evaluating the type of personal data involved, how it will be used, who will access it, and how long it will be retained. If your organization has a PIA process in place, this is when it should be initiated and completed.

Feasibility Analysis

Not everything that users want is technically or operationally realistic. A feasibility analysis puts the requirements through a practical lens and asks: Can we actually do this? Are the necessary data sources accessible and of sufficient quality? Do we have the tooling, skills, and platform support to deliver what's being asked?

There are several angles to consider when assessing feasibility:

- **Technical**: Whether the infrastructure, systems, and architecture can support what is being proposed.
- **Data**: Whether the required data exists, is accessible, and meets the necessary quality thresholds.
- **Operational**: Whether business processes and teams are ready to adopt and sustain the solution.
- **Organizational**: Whether the right people, roles, and governance structures are in place.
- **Security and compliance**: Whether legal, regulatory, and privacy constraints can be respected.
- **Financial**: whether the available budget aligns with the projected cost to build and maintain the product.

This is the moment when architects, engineers, governance leads, and compliance teams weigh in. Their input helps clarify what is achievable now, what might need to be simplified, and what should be deferred to a future iteration.

Sprint Prioritization

Most data products cannot be built in one go. Sprint prioritization involves breaking down the long list of possible requirements into smaller, manageable chunks that can be delivered incrementally. This often starts with feature prioritization, which involves identifying what functionality is most critical to deliver first, but it can also include scoping initial data sources, integrations, or user experiences. Prioritization typically considers three core factors: business impact, technical complexity, and user urgency.

A strong sprint prioritization process helps teams stay focused and deliver value early. It also sets the stage for iteration, enabling teams to learn from what works and refine the data product continuously. This is especially important for data products that involve analytics, AI, or advanced data-driven use cases, where early assumptions often change once the data is explored more deeply. While the earlier Figure 4 in this section outlines the data product lifecycle as a structured sequence, it is worth noting that most successful teams adopt Agile principles. Many of these steps are revisited or refined across multiple sprints, rather than treated as a rigid waterfall.

2.1.3. Design

In the design phase, a concrete blueprint for what will be built is created. It bridges the gap between user needs and technical implementation, laying the foundation for development. This is the moment when abstract ideas and requirements become real structures, expressed in tables, pipelines, access controls, interfaces, and more.

- **Data Model:** Even at the design stage, it helps to think about data conceptually, before tying yourself to specific fields in existing systems. A good data model defines the key entities, attributes, and relationships that the product should include. Doing this early makes everything easier later: it guides infrastructure, shapes data quality rules, and helps ensure users interpret the data correctly. The best practice is to document the critical attributes, their relationships, and their definitions. With today's AI tools, you can sketch a solid first draft in a matter of minutes. If your organization has an enterprise data model, now is the time to align with it to improve interoperability and future reuse.

- **Data and Solution Architecture:** The technical blueprint for what you're about to build. It covers how data moves, how systems connect, and how the overall solution is structured. That typically includes defining storage layers, data ingestion and transformation patterns, orchestration logic, and whether flows run in batch or in real time. If you have a solid architecture, you write it down. Like blueprints for a building, it makes sure what you're creating is strong and built to last.

- **Data Quality and Integrity:** This is your chance to build data quality in by design. It may seem obvious to include it here, but in my experience, it's one of the most overlooked steps. This is where you determine what quality controls and integrity checks the product needs. That includes things like allowable values, referential integrity, threshold checks, and business rules. You plan where errors get caught and how they get handled. This matters because without trust, no one will use it. And without usage, there's no impact. Quality is what makes the product reliable, usable, and worth building in the first place.

- **Metadata Design:** This step is not yet about capturing every piece of metadata, but about setting the stage for how it will be handled later. At this point, it's helpful to define at least the logical business definitions of your critical data attributes, in line with the data model step that we defined earlier. But more importantly, you're making decisions about which types of metadata you care about, how you plan to capture them, and what level of automation will be built in. This is especially relevant now, with increased attention on concepts like data observability. For example, if timeliness, volume, or schema changes are important, this is the time to figure out how to track those through automated logging or platform hooks. Thinking this through during design can save a lot of headaches later.

- **Data Protection and Security:** This step focuses on ensuring that the product complies with data protection policies and security expectations. This may include data classification, role-based access control, data masking, encryption, anonymization, and audit logging. Designing security upfront prevents delays, avoids risk exposure, and shows maturity. Involving legal, privacy, and security teams at this stage makes it easier to embed controls into the product rather than bolt them on later. Especially when dealing with personal or sensitive data, this part of the design process is (or should be) non-negotiable.

- **Data Retention:** Defines how long different types of data are stored, when they are archived, and when they are deleted.[1] Business needs, legal requirements, system constraints, and estimated costs typically inform these decisions. There are at least three good reasons to think this through. First, you don't want to lose important data by accident, so you need to make sure it's stored or backed up appropriately. Second, storing large volumes of data can get expensive, so unless there's a good reason, you shouldn't keep everything forever. And third, you may be legally required to either delete data after a certain time or retain it for a minimum period.

- **User Experience:** Some data products include user interfaces, such as dashboards, portals, or internal tools. In some cases, a data product might simply be a dataset available through an API or file drop, with no real interface at all. But when there is a UI or UX dimension to it, this is the step to think through what that experience should look and feel like. A well-designed interface can boost adoption, reduce support needs, and make the product more effective. That's true even for internal tools. That said, I'm not a dashboard or visualization expert, and there are already great books and resources out there for that.

---

[1] See (Gagliardi 2023).

This book won't focus much on UI/UX design, but it's still an important step in the overall journey for some data products.

- **Design Blueprint:** Across all of these design components, it can really help to keep a simple data product blueprint on hand as you work. It gives you one place to bring the key ideas together as they evolve from planning through analysis to detailed design. It can be incredibly helpful (and fun!) to organize a workshop around this blueprint, bringing the right cross-functional stakeholders together to complete the template in a focused two- or three-hour working session. Figure 7 shows a straightforward template you can start with, and Figure 8 includes a completed example for the Finance Reconciliation Engine data product that we will continue using throughout the rest of this book.

Data Product: *Data Product Name*

Purpose and Objectives	Explains what the data product aims to achieve and why it matters.
Supported Business Use Cases and Value Hypothesis	Describes the business processes and use cases supported and the value the product is expected to deliver.
Key Stakeholders	Lists the main people involved and their role or interest in the data product.
Risks or Assumptions	Highlights known risks and key assumptions that could affect delivery.

Scope and Requirements	
Data and Data Sources	What (raw) data is needed, and what are its requirements for completeness, granularity, frequency, and quality?
Integration and Storage	How will the data be ingested and where will it be stored, including interface or storage layer considerations?
Cleansing and Curation	What checks, processing, and quality rules must be applied to make the data usable and trustworthy?
Transformation and Enrichment	What transformations, logic, analytics, or AI must be applied to enhance the data product?
Consumption and Usage	Who will use the data, in what format or tool, and whether dashboards, exports, or APIs are required?

Figure 7 – Template for a Data Product Design Blueprint.

Data Product: *Finance Reconciliation Engine*

Purpose and Objectives	Automate, standardize, and streamline the reconciliation of financial transactions across ERP systems, bank statements, and payment processor feeds. It exists to eliminate manual effort, reduce reconciliation errors, shorten the month-end close, and ensure that financial data is accurate, complete, and audit-ready. The objective is to provide a single, trusted, continuously updated view of reconciled transactions for Finance, Accounting, and Audit teams.
Supported Business Use Cases and Value Hypothesis	**Primary Use Cases:** • Month-end close: Automate matching logic and exception handling to shorten close cycles and reduce manual work. • Cash application and collections: Ensure customer payments are captured accurately and on time to prevent missed or delayed revenue. • Audit and compliance reporting: Provide a traceable, transparent record of reconciliations for internal audit and external regulators. **Value Hypotheses:** • 5,000+ hours of manual effort removed annually. • 3–4 days faster month-end close. • Prevention of 0.1–0.2% revenue leakage from missed or delayed payments. • Reduced risk exposure.
Key Stakeholders	• **Product Owner:** Director of Finance Operations • **Data Product Manager:** Finance Data Enablement Lead • **Technical Lead/Data Engineer:** Finance IT Integration Team • **Data Steward:** Finance Data Governance Representative • **Consumers:** Global Finance Operations; Regional Accounting Teams; Internal Audit; Corporate Compliance; Treasury
Risks or Assumptions	**Assumptions:** • Consistent access to bank statements and payment processor data feeds. • ERP and finance systems have the necessary transaction-level data. • Finance teams commit to adopting the new automated workflow. **Risks:** • Delays in integrating external third-party feeds. • Business rules may require frequent adjustments during early adoption. • Data quality issues in upstream systems. • Teams may continue using manual spreadsheets.

Scope and Requirements

Data and Data Sources	**Required Data Inputs:** • ERP general ledger and subledger transactions. • Bank statements (daily feed). • Payment processor files (Stripe, Adyen, PayPal, etc.). • Chargebacks, refunds, and adjustments. • Master data for accounts, customers, and payment types. **Data Requirements:** • Completeness: must include all daily transactions. • Granularity: transaction-level. • Frequency: daily with an intraday refresh option. • Quality: >99% match accuracy target.
Integration and Storage	• Data will be ingested using AWS Glue jobs, S3 storage, and event-driven updates where available. • Raw data stored in S3; curated and reconciled data stored in Redshift. • API integration for bank and payment processor data where possible; secure file transfer fallback. • Staging layer supports versioning, reprocessing, and delta ingestion.
Cleansing and Curation	• Apply validation rules (schema checks, duplicate detection, balance checks). • Normalize formats across banks and processors. • Run automated matching logic with configurable tolerances. • Flag exceptions and route them to a dedicated review queue. • Apply referential checks against master data.
Transformation and Enrichment	• Apply deterministic and fuzzy matching algorithms. • Generate reconciliation status flags (matched, unmatched, pending). • Create exception reason codes for downstream processing. • Produce enriched output dataset containing: matched pairs, unmatched transactions, confidence scores, audit trail IDs. • Include metadata fields for traceability, such as lineage and processing timestamps.
Consumption and Usage	**Primary Consumers:** Finance Operations, Accounting, Audit, Treasury **Consumption Methods:** • SQL view through Redshift. • Reconciliation API for system-to-system consumption. • Prebuilt exception reports (CSV/JSON exports). • Dashboard views for close-cycle monitoring. **User Needs:** • Ability to drill into unmatched transactions. • Daily freshness SLAs. • Clear auditability for compliance purposes.

Figure 8 – Completed data product design blueprint template for a data product "Finance Reconciliation Engine."

2.1.4. Build

This phase is where design becomes reality. The build phase involves the actual development work of ingesting, processing, transforming, and preparing the data product.

- **Data Ingestion and Integration:** This step involves bringing data from the appropriate systems. That typically means setting up data pipelines—automated, repeatable processes that move data from source systems into target storage or processing layers—to ingest source data, whether from internal platforms like ERP or CRM systems, external sources such as third-party APIs, or flat files. Integration often involves joining multiple systems, handling schema mismatches, and creating stable interfaces that work long-term. Good ingestion and integration ensure that data arrives consistently and in the expected format. It's also where you establish the foundations of traceability and observability. Done right, it's repeatable, robust, and easy to monitor, supporting long-term scale and reliability.

- **Data Curation:** This is where we ensure that the data is "fit for purpose." Data curation includes initial cleaning, validation, standardization, and restructuring. This is not yet about analytics or adding features; rather, it is about ensuring the data is accurate, interpretable, and usable. You can think of this step as aligning with what is often referred to as the bronze-to-silver layer transition in a medallion architecture. Raw, ingested data (bronze) is cleaned, standardized, and refined into a higher-quality, analysis-ready form (silver). In many modern data stacks, this step helps enforce consistency and provides the dependable foundation that later analytical features and business usage will rely on.

- **Data Enrichment:** This is the point in the lifecycle where the product transitions from silver to gold. The data is already cleaned and standardized; now it is enriched, aggregated, and purpose-built. This may include advanced calculations, custom KPIs, segmentation flags, predictive model outputs, or any derived values designed to support specific decisions or business use cases.

- **Data Processing and Storage:** Processing and storage are not separate steps. They are foundational across parts of the build phase. As data is ingested, curated, and enriched, it must be processed and stored in ways that support performance, reliability, and scalability. This ensures that those needs are met holistically across the entire data product. This is where you build a deliberately designed architecture with the right storage layers, efficient compute, and the ability to scale as needed. Depending on the product, the processed data may ultimately live in a data lake, a data warehouse, an operational store, or a BI environment.

- **Data Consumption and Distribution:** Now that the data is ready, it needs to be made accessible. This may include enabling query access, setting up API endpoints, building pipelines to downstream tools, or loading data into dashboards or visual layers. You're creating the final delivery path so the product is usable in practice. A strong distribution plan ensures that the right people get the right data in the right way. It also includes entitlements, access control, and documentation to guide usage. When done poorly, teams build great data products that nobody knows how—or is allowed—to use.

- **Metadata Creation:** This is where metadata gets captured and surfaced. That includes basic structural metadata such as data types and field names, but may also include more advanced context such as lineage, quality scores, and update timestamps. This step depends on good planning during the design phase. Much of this metadata capture can and should be automated. Build-time scripts, data observability tools, and platform plugins can all help with this.

2.1.5. Deployment

Deployment is the phase where the data product goes live. After all the planning, analysis, design, and build work, this is where the product becomes usable in production.

- **Testing:** Before deployment, the product must be tested. This includes functional testing (Does it do what it should?), performance testing (Does it run fast and reliably?), and quality testing (Is the data correct and complete?). Without proper testing, issues will likely surface in production, where they're much harder to fix.

- **Deployment to Production:** Once tested, the product is deployed into the production environment. This step includes setting up pipelines, access controls, alerts, and scheduling, depending on what the product needs. The goal is stability; users should be able to access and rely on the product without surprises.

- **Process Documentation:** This is where you document how the product runs operationally. What jobs need to be monitored? Where do logs go? What should teams check when something fails? These operational procedures help keep the product running smoothly and make troubleshooting easier later. This is also a key enabler for data governance and ownership. Defining who owns the process and how it works avoids reliance on tribal knowledge and ensures long-term accountability.

- **Metadata Harvesting:** Metadata should be collected automatically during and after deployment. This may include lineage, data quality metrics, refresh times, and usage logs. What was planned and designed earlier in the lifecycle now needs to be executed. Any metadata pipelines or native harvesting options must be set up so that this information is continuously captured and made available from day one.

- **Support and Handover:** Even if the product is technically live, it's not fully deployed until users and support teams know how to use it and maintain it. This step includes walkthroughs, training, documentation, and, if needed, setting up support channels.

2.1.6. Usage

This phase is about putting the data product to work. After deployment, the focus shifts to how users actually find, access, and benefit from the product. Usage is what turns a data product from an asset into impact.

- **Data Catalog Publication:** Publishing to the data catalog is what makes the product findable. It allows users across the organization to search, discover, and understand what the product is, what it contains, and how to use it. This should build on metadata designed and captured earlier in the lifecycle, and hence should not require any extra heavy lifting at this point.

- **Access Control and Provisioning:** This is when users actually start requesting access. Ideally, you've already planned access rules in earlier phases, but now they get implemented in practice. Best practice here is to use role-based access controls, granting access based on a person's role or department, and, if needed, column-level and row-level controls for sensitive fields. That helps avoid manual approvals and improves security and scalability.

- **User Training:** Depending on the complexity of the data product, some level of training may be helpful. This can take many forms: a short video walkthrough, a simple PDF guide, or a live session. What matters is that new users can understand what the product is for, how to use it, and where to go for help. Usage will stall if people are confused or hesitant.

- **Consumption and Value Tracking:** This is the moment the product starts delivering value. Consumption might happen through dashboards, APIs, queries, or exports. The goal is for the product to be actively used in decision-making, reporting, analysis, or automation. Back in the planning and requirements phase, you defined the value this product should deliver. Now is the time to track it. There are a few categories of KPIs to consider. First, usage metrics like the number of users, queries, or downloads. Second, feedback-based metrics like user satisfaction or perceived usefulness. And third, business impact measures tied to the original use cases, such as improved conversion rates, lower churn, or increased revenue. We'll come back to value tracking and business case validation later in the book (see Section 2.2. Value Quantification and Business Case).

- **Cost Monitoring and Billing:** In cloud environments, it's especially important to monitor costs for storage, compute, and usage. In some organizations, this also includes internal chargebacks or showbacks to encourage responsible usage. You don't always need to pass these costs through to users, but someone should be watching. High usage might mean success or inefficiency.

- **Feedback Management:** Feedback helps the product evolve. This step involves collecting user input, identifying pain points, and prioritizing improvements. It closes the loop and ensures the product continues to meet real-world needs.

2.1.7. Maintenance

Once a data product is live, it needs care. Maintenance is about keeping things running smoothly, securely, and reliably. This phase ensures that the product stays healthy and usable over time.

- **Operations and Monitoring:** You need to monitor pipelines, storage, compute usage, and performance. This helps spot failures early, avoid downtime, and make sure the product scales as usage grows. Just as with any software product, data products may need code updates (e.g., new logic or bug fixes), dependency updates (e.g., library or infrastructure component updates), or infrastructure tweaks. DevOps refers to the practices and tooling that enable automated deployments, integration, and monitoring. A good DevOps setup makes this easier, with automated deployments and rollback options if something breaks.

- **Data Policies and Standards Compliance:** As part of broader data governance, ensure the data product continues to comply with relevant data policies. That includes privacy, security, naming conventions, retention, and classification. For data products, a best practice is to define a minimal set of certification or validation standards that verify compliance with policies and requirements. We'll cover this in more detail in Section 2.3.4. Certification of Data Products.

- **Data Quality Control and Incident Management:** If a data product needs to be reliable and trustworthy, then data quality must be controlled throughout its lifecycle. These checks can be automated, run as regular samples, or embedded in observability tooling. In any case, there needs to be some kind of control in place to confirm the data remains fit for purpose. Someone should be responsible for acting when quality issues are detected. Make sure users know how to report issues, and set up clear workflows for triage, resolution, and communication.

- **Change Management:** If you're serious about treating data as a product, then it follows that your product today may not meet tomorrow's needs. Just as cars or clothes can evolve, requirements can, and the product must evolve with them. Change management involves actively evaluating and implementing necessary changes. This includes responding to feedback and known issues, as well as taking a step back regularly to assess whether the product still delivers on its intended value.

2.1.8. Demise

At some point, a data product reaches the end of its useful life. The demise phase ensures that this happens in a controlled, responsible way. Knowing when to retire a product is just as important as knowing when to create one. It helps rationalize the data landscape, reduce unnecessary costs, and maintain clarity around what's still active and supported. But as you do so, it's essential to ensure that anyone who depends on the product is properly informed, supported, or transitioned.

- **Impact Analysis:** Before retiring a product, assess how it's being used. Are there dashboards, pipelines, or teams that depend on it? You need to understand the downstream impact to avoid breaking anything unexpectedly.

- **Disposition Plan:** Once you know the impact, define how the product will be phased out. This might include timelines, communication plans, and transition steps to alternatives. The goal is to reduce disruption.

- **Archival:** If the product contains important historical data, archive it appropriately. That includes storing it in a cost-effective location, labeling it clearly, and ensuring access for auditing or future analysis.

- **Shutdown:** Finally, deactivate the pipelines, access permissions, and infrastructure components. This step should fully retire the product from active use and stop any related costs or risks.

2.2. Value Quantification and Business Case

Before committing resources to design, build, and operate a data product, it's critical to understand not only what it will do but also why it matters. In this chapter, we introduce a simple, reusable business case template that can be applied to any data product (see Figure 9). The purpose of this template is straightforward: to help you clearly articulate the value a data product is expected to deliver, capture its costs, and evaluate its overall financial impact. Whether you are seeking investment approval, prioritizing competing initiatives, or ensuring ongoing accountability, this structure helps you make decisions on a sound basis.

Data Product Business Case Framework

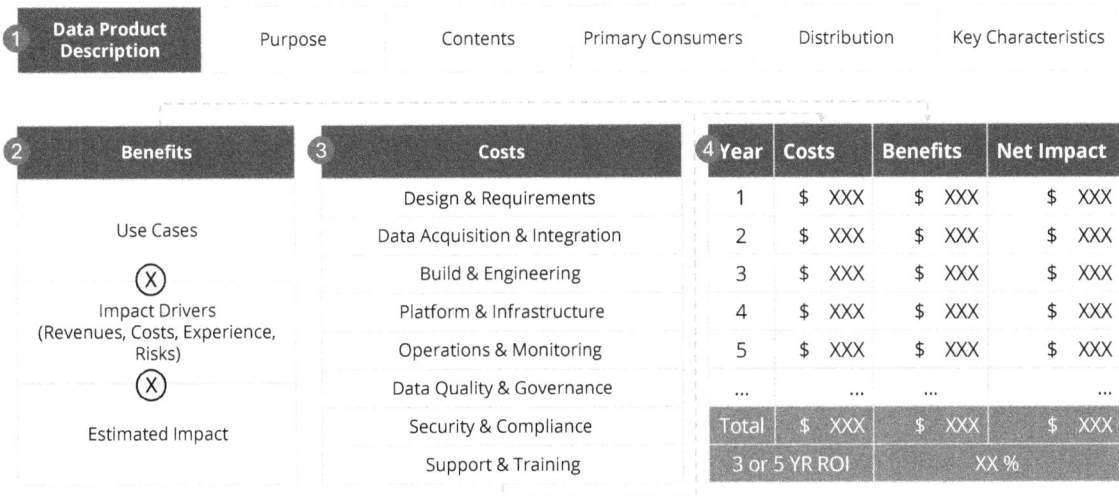

1 **Data Product Description**	Purpose	Contents	Primary Consumers	Distribution	Key Characteristics

2 Benefits	**3 Costs**	**4 Year**	**Costs**	**Benefits**	**Net Impact**
Use Cases	Design & Requirements	1	$ XXX	$ XXX	$ XXX
(X)	Data Acquisition & Integration	2	$ XXX	$ XXX	$ XXX
Impact Drivers	Build & Engineering	3	$ XXX	$ XXX	$ XXX
(Revenues, Costs, Experience, Risks)	Platform & Infrastructure	4	$ XXX	$ XXX	$ XXX
(X)	Operations & Monitoring	5	$ XXX	$ XXX	$ XXX
	Data Quality & Governance	...	...	...	...
Estimated Impact	Security & Compliance	Total	$ XXX	$ XXX	$ XXX
	Support & Training	3 or 5 YR ROI		XX %	

Figure 9 – Financial business case framework for data products.

The template contains four core components:

1. **Data Product Description**: A concise overview of what the data product is, what data it contains, how it works, and which audiences will use it. This sets the stage and ensures everyone shares a common understanding of the asset.

2. **Benefits Assessment**: A structured breakdown of how the product will deliver value, linked to specific use cases and mapped to the four main value levers: revenue uplift, cost efficiency, customer/employee experience, and risk mitigation.

3. **Cost Estimate/Total Cost of Ownership (TCO)**: A full accounting of the expected costs over the life of the product, including build, operations, licensing, maintenance, enhancements, governance, and support.

4. **Financial Case and Metrics**: The final piece that brings the benefits and costs together into clear business case metrics, such as ROI, payback period, and net annual value.

2.2.1. Data Product Description

The first part of the business case template is the Data Product Description. It makes sure everyone understands what the product is and how it will be used. We cover five components here: the purpose, the contents, the primary consumers, the distribution, and the key characteristics. See Figure 10 for the template and an illustrative example.

We will use the Finance Reconciliation Engine as our running example. Imagine a global retail company with about four billion dollars in annual revenue, operating across many markets and channels. Financial reconciliation matters because it checks that what is in the ERP and ledgers matches what appears in bank statements, payment processor files, and other external records. If you skip this, cash can be misstated, duplicate or missing entries go unnoticed, and audits and regulatory filings are put at risk. It can also directly lead to missed revenues, for example, when customer payments are made but not detected and therefore never collected.

For years, the finance team struggled to reconcile data across their ERP, multiple payment processors, and bank statements. Much of the work was manual in spreadsheets and via email, leading to errors and delays, and the month-end close often dragged on.

Data Product Description	
Element	**Details**
Purpose	Automate and standardize the reconciliation of financial transactions across multiple systems, reducing manual effort, improving accuracy, and ensuring timely financial reporting.
Contents	Processed and matched transaction records from ERP, payment processors, bank statements, and subsidiary ledgers; reconciliation status flags; unmatched transaction queues; audit logs.
Primary Consumers	Finance operations teams, accounting staff, internal audit, compliance officers, and financial controllers.
Distribution	Accessible via a secure web portal for finance teams; API access for integration into ERP and accounting software; scheduled delivery of reconciliation reports to stakeholders.
Key Characteristics	High data accuracy (>99% match rate); automated matching rules with configurable tolerances; real-time status updates; full audit trail; compliance-ready reporting formats; integration with major ERP systems.

Figure 10 – Data product description template.

The Finance Reconciliation Engine was built to fix this. It pulls transaction records from all major sources, runs automated matching with configurable tolerances, flags exceptions, and produces near real-time reconciliation reports. Finance, accounting, and audit teams access it through a secure portal or AP1. Key characteristics include high match accuracy, full audit trails, clear ownership, and compliance-ready outputs. We will keep using this example as we walk through the business case template in the next sections.

2.2.2. Benefits

Now that we've introduced the Finance Reconciliation Engine as an example data product, it's time to turn to the part that most decision-makers care about most: why it matters. A business case only becomes compelling when it clearly shows (and quantifies) the impact a data product can have. Any good business case must ultimately tie back to one or more of the following four value levers:

- **Increased Revenue**: The most direct way data products create value is by enabling new or improved revenue streams. That can happen in a few ways. A strong data product might support better pricing decisions, more personalized marketing, or more effective sales targeting. These aren't abstract outcomes. They lead to more closed deals, higher customer conversion, and larger average purchases. More strategically, data products can also power innovation. They can serve as platforms for building AI-driven products, optimizing product development, or identifying new customer segments. For example, a data product that delivers accurate, well-segmented customer behavior data might support both today's sales team and tomorrow's product team. It creates a foundation for both immediate wins and future growth.

- **Reduced Cost**: Reducing cost can be one of the clearest, most measurable benefits of data products. A major lever here is rationalizing the data and systems landscape. Most companies have redundant reports, overlapping systems, and multiple sources managing the same data. Each of those carries a cost in terms of licensing, maintenance, infrastructure, or human labor. By consolidating and replacing overlapping sources with well-defined data products, you can materially reduce those costs. Additionally, well-structured data products reduce the time analysts and data scientists spend searching for data, cleaning it, double-checking its accuracy, and preparing it for usage. That can add up to a lot of hours saved across large teams. Working across a couple of globally leading companies over the last few years, data users reported spending well over 50% of their time looking for, obtaining access to, and then cleaning and preparing the data. Data products can significantly reduce this manual time and effort. Similarly, when operational workflows are powered by consistent data products (for example, automated billing, claims processing, or lead routing), the automation itself becomes more efficient, scalable, and less error-prone. Savings such as these help the bottom line and free up time and resources for higher-value activities.

- **Enhanced Customer or Employee Experience**: Experience for both customers and employees is an often overlooked but increasingly important value driver. And data products play a critical role. From a customer perspective, high-quality data products support faster, more relevant, and more consistent interactions. If your contact center, CRM, and website all draw from the same trusted product master or customer profile data product, customers will notice. Fewer mistakes. Fewer delays. Fewer transfers between departments. From an employee perspective, data products reduce frustration and improve productivity. When teams can easily find and trust the data they need, they spend less time in meetings, chasing down owners, or doing rework. The result is smoother collaboration, faster onboarding, and more empowered decision-making. A great experience tends to amplify other value levers. Customers who enjoy consistent service are more loyal. Employees who have what they need do better work. Over time, this shows up in both revenue and cost metrics, but even in the short term, it's a meaningful standalone benefit.

- **Risk Mitigation and Reputation Protection:** Finally, data products are one of the most powerful tools for reducing data-related risks. With traditional fragmented systems, it's hard to know who owns which data, where sensitive fields live, and whether you're compliant with regulations like GDPR or HIPAA. Data products, by contrast, are defined, described, and monitored. They are the perfect units for attaching controls, classifying data, and enforcing policies. As we'll explore later in the book, a best practice is to establish data product certification standards: lightweight checklists or assessments that verify the product meets required privacy, security, and compliance criteria. These standards might include requirements for classification, access controls, PII masking, audit logging, and more. If something goes wrong, such as a breach, an audit, or a customer data issue, data products give you a clearer picture of what's affected, who's responsible, and how to respond. That's real risk mitigation. In industries where data risk carries financial or reputational consequences, this is often one of the most tangible value levers. In some cases, avoiding even one compliance failure or regulatory penalty pays for the entire investment in the data product approach.

Before we jump straight from a data product to business value, it's important to make one thing clear: data products by themselves don't generate value. They only do so when they power specific use cases: the business processes, decisions, or workflows that depend on the data product to run more effectively. A use case is essentially the bridge between the data product and the value levers; it defines how the data is applied and where the impact shows up.

For the Finance Reconciliation Engine, some of the critical use cases include:

- **Month-end close process**: Speeding up the reconciliation between ERP records, bank statements, and payment processor files to shorten closing cycles.

- **Cash application and collections**: Ensuring incoming payments are matched correctly so that no revenue goes missing and customer balances remain accurate.

- **Audit and compliance reporting**: Providing reliable, auditable records to meet external regulatory requirements and reduce risk during inspections.

With these use cases defined, we can now connect them to the four value levers and show exactly how the Finance Reconciliation Engine drives tangible impact. In practice, a single use case can affect multiple levers, but for simplicity, in this example, we'll highlight just the primary driver for each (see Table 8).

You can take the template we're building here and very easily translate it into an Excel file or similar tool. From there, you can make the benefit modeling as simple or as sophisticated as you want. In practice, many estimates are not exact sciences, and they never will be. Even when the link between a data product and a business outcome seems relatively clear, there are often cases where the impact is real but less direct. That's why it helps to keep use cases as the anchor: define the use cases, connect them to benefit drivers, and then apply estimation techniques.

Use Case	Primary Benefit Driver	Benefit Description (Quantified)
Month-end close	Cost Efficiency	Automating reconciliation reduces manual effort and rework, cutting overtime and shortening the close by ~3 days. This saves ~5,000 hours annually across global finance teams, worth about $400K–$500K per year.
Cash application and collections	Revenue Uptick	Ensures incoming payments are captured accurately and on time. Prevents 0.1–0.2% of revenue from being missed or delayed, equivalent to $4M–$8M annually. Assuming a 15% net margin, the incremental profit impact is about $900K annually ($6M × 15%).
Audit and compliance reporting	Risk Mitigation	Audit teams and regulators get direct access to clean, traceable records. This reduces audit prep time by 30% and avoids at least one potential compliance penalty every three years, together valued at about $1M annually.

Table 8 – Summary of key benefits for the Data Reconciliation Engine data product.

One very practical approach is to model ranges or scenarios (e.g., low/medium/high) by assessing how directly the data product enables the use case. At the "high" end, the use case is essentially impossible without the data product. At the "low" end, the use case would still work mostly as is, but the data product makes it more efficient or reliable. These confidence levels give you a way to reflect uncertainty while still keeping the business case grounded.

In our example, this is exactly how we arrived at the quantified benefits of the Finance Reconciliation Engine. For cash application and collections, the low scenario assumed that 0.1% of revenue would otherwise be missed, while the high scenario assumed 0.2%. The midpoint and practical average estimate are 0.15%. With the company's annual revenue of $4B, this translates to a potential capture of $6M in revenue ($4B × 0.15%).

However, this figure reflects the top-line revenue impact. To understand the effect on the bottom line, you need to apply the company's profit margin, since not every dollar of revenue flows directly into profit (you'd be surprised how often this mistake is made). If we assume a 15% net profit margin, the incremental profit impact is about $900K annually ($6M × 15%). This step of adjusting gross revenue impacts to net profit is critical for making a business case credible and comparable to other investments competing for funding.

It's important to note that data teams cannot (and should not) claim every dollar of value created. The business functions that operate and execute the processes also need to capture a share of the benefits, since they are critical in turning the data foundation into actual outcomes. In my experience, very few cases attribute more than 50% of benefits to data teams, and in many cases, it is closer to 10–25%. The estimates provided in this section already reflect such a conservative allocation, so we don't have to incorporate them further. But to make this concrete, consider a next-best-action use case in which advanced analytics recommends the best product to offer a customer at a given moment. If the total value of that use case is estimated at $5M, it would not be credible for the data team to claim the entire $5M. Business teams running the campaigns or customer interactions must also take credit. A more realistic approach would be to attribute perhaps 25% of the value ($1.25M) to the data foundations, with the remainder owned by the front-line functions. This type of shared attribution avoids turf wars and ensures a collaborative environment, which is absolutely essential for the success of data products.

2.2.3. Costs

Now that we have covered the benefits side, the next step is to look at the costs of building and maintaining a data product. Whereas the revenue and benefit estimates in the previous section are often more of an art, involving assumptions, ranges, and confidence levels, the costs are generally more concrete. While not every detail will be known upfront, most organizations should be able to arrive at a reasonably precise approximation of the total cost of ownership (TCO). We will need to present costs on the same basis (say, annual) as benefits to be able to relate them.

Although the exact structure will differ by organization (depending on tools, vendor agreements, internal rates, allocation mechanisms, etc.), most data products share a consistent set of cost categories. These include both one-time investments and recurring operating costs.

There are various ways to present and group these costs. To make this more tangible, we'll use a lifecycle view, tying them roughly to the natural stages of a data product's journey:

- **Design and Requirements:** This covers the upfront work of defining what the data product will be. It includes scoping, requirements gathering, building data models, drafting user stories, and aligning with business processes. The costs here are mostly people-driven, for example, through business analysts, architects, and data product managers, but could also include specialized design tools or workshops.

- **Data Acquisition (Internal and Third-Party):** No data product exists without data. This category covers sourcing raw materials: onboarding internal datasets into pipelines, paying for external feeds or APIs, and ensuring proper licensing for third-party datasets. In many organizations, this is a significant and recurring line item.

- **Build and Engineering:** This is where the data product is actually created. Costs here include developing ingestion pipelines, transformation logic, APIs, and user interfaces, as well as testing and deployment. Both engineering labor and technology tools (e.g., orchestration frameworks, CI/CD platforms) belong here.

- **Run and Operate:** Once built, the product needs to run reliably. This category captures cloud infrastructure (compute, storage, hosting), ongoing platform/tool licensing (ETL, data quality, visualization), DevOps work, and system monitoring. It's the largest recurring bucket for many organizations.

- **Data Quality and Governance:** Good data products are and stay trustworthy. This requires initial and ongoing data quality checks, issue remediation, metadata management, stewardship activities, and use of governance tools such as data catalogs or lineage platforms. Both automation and human stewardship fall into this category.

- **Security and Compliance:** Data products must be protected and compliant, wherever possible, "by design." Costs here include identity and access management, encryption, data masking, audit logging, regulatory compliance monitoring (e.g., GDPR, HIPAA), and, in some cases, third-party security certifications.

- **Enhancements and Evolution:** Finally, no data product is ever "finished." Over time, new user needs emerge, more automation becomes possible, and business processes change. This category budgets for iterative improvements, scaling, retraining of models where applicable, and adding new features that extend the product's usefulness.

Having introduced the key cost categories, Table 9 below shows how they map out in practice for our running example.

Category	Cost Item	Costing Rationale	Type	Annualized Estimate
Design and Requirements	Business analyst effort	300 hours @ $100/hour, amortized over three years	One-off	$30,000
	Data architect effort	100 hours @ $150/hour	One-off	$5,000
Data Acquisition and Integration	Third-party bank feeds/APIs	Vendor subscription	Recurring	$30,000
	Internal system integration	100 hours @ $150/hour	One-off	$15,000
Build and Engineering	Initial engineering build	800 hours @ $150/hour = $120K	One-off	$120,000
	Incremental feature engineering	300 hours @ $150/hour	One-off	$45,000
	User-requested tuning	100 hours @ $200/hour	One-off	$20,000
Platform and Infrastructure	Cloud compute and storage	~10M monthly transactions @ cloud rates	Recurring	$100,000
	ETL/ELT platform license	$1.25M annual license ÷ 25 products = $50K allocation	Recurring	$50,000
	Reporting/visualization tool	$125K license ÷ 25 products = $5K allocation	Recurring	$5,000
Operations and Monitoring	DevOps effort	500 hours @ $130/hour	Recurring	$65,000
	Reconciliation monitoring and QA	300 hours @ $150/hour	Recurring	$45,000
Data Quality and Governance	Data catalog license allocation	$250K annual license ÷ 25 products = $10K allocation	Recurring	$10,000
	Data quality tooling allocation	$75K annual license ÷ 25 products = $3K allocation	Recurring	$3,000
	Data steward effort	0.25 FTE, 500 hours/year @ $80/hour	Recurring	$40,000
Security and Compliance	Identity and Access Mgmt allocation	$500K IAM service ÷ 25 products = $20K allocation	Recurring	$20,000
	Encryption and masking allocation	$375K shared infra ÷ 25 products = $15K allocation	Recurring	$15,000
	Audit logging and compliance	50 hours security analyst @ $175/hour	Recurring	$8,750
Support and Training	User onboarding and documentation	Training sessions, guides, and support materials (~80 hours @ $100/hour)	Recurring	$8,000

Table 9 – Estimated costs for the Financial Reconciliation Engine.

When you look at the table, a few things may stand out. Some cost items can be attributed directly to the data product itself. For instance, in the design and build categories, we can estimate the time spent by business analysts or data architects quite precisely in hours and rates. Other items are harder to pin to a single product. Examples include the data catalog license, data quality tooling, IAM services, or shared security infrastructure. These are foundational capabilities that span many products, so their costs must be allocated back in some way.

There are different ways to do this in practice, for example, by the number of users supported, by usage volume, or by simply dividing across the portfolio of data products. To keep this example simple and in line with the focus of this book, we use the last approach. Throughout the table, you will see references to a portfolio of 25 data products, with costs from shared infrastructure or tooling divided equally across them. This gives us a clear, consistent way to show the total cost of ownership for a single product.

2.2.4. Financial Summary and ROI

Now that we have walked through both the benefits and the costs of the Finance Reconciliation Engine, the next step is to bring everything together into a single view. This is where the business case becomes truly actionable: we align the projected benefits and the estimated costs on a comparable basis so that management can quickly see the return on investment.

On the benefits side, we estimated:

- Cost efficiency savings of about $400K–$500K per year from shorter month-end close.
- Revenue uplift of $4M–$8M per year from more accurate and timely cash application, generating ~$900k incremental profit.
- Risk mitigation and compliance benefits valued at about $1M per year.

On the cost side, we estimated:

- One-off development and build costs of about $235,000.
- Recurring annual costs of about $399,750 for operations, licensing, infrastructure, and governance.

If we bring this together, the financial profile looks as follows:

Year(s)	Costs (One-off + Recurring)	Benefits	Net Impact
1	$ 634,750	$ 0	$ (634,750)
2	$ 399,750	$ 2,350,000	$ 1,950,250
3	$ 399,750	$ 2,350,000	$ 1,950,250
1+2+3	$ 1,434,250	$ 4,700,000	$ 3,265,750

Table 10 – Cost-benefit analysis table for the Financial Recommendation Engine.

The payback period for this investment is early in Year 2, meaning the upfront development cost is recovered quickly and the recurring benefits begin to outweigh ongoing costs soon after launch. Over a three-year horizon (ignoring discounting), the total investment is approximately $1.43M, while total benefits amount to about $4.70M, resulting in a net benefit of roughly $3.27M. This equates to a three-year ROI of approximately 225–230%.

This illustrates why strong data products tend to stand out: the financial return is both fast and substantial. As a rule of thumb, data products should break even within one to two years, and the three- to five-year ROI should not be marginal; it should be obvious, with multiples of 2x, 3x, or more. A business case that only shows 5% net return over several years is not compelling, given the effort, risk, and change management required.

From my experience, data products and data assets with business cases built this way often deliver average ROI multiples in the 10x to 20x range. While benefits are always subject to estimation and some uncertainty, the direction is clear: when done right, the return profile should leave no doubt.

2.3. Data Product Blueprints and Architectural Guidelines

In the previous sections, we looked at the data product lifecycle and how to build a strong business case. That sets the stage for the next step: designing and building a data product.

2.3.1. Reference Data Architecture

The natural question becomes: where do we start? A powerful way to avoid reinventing the wheel every time is to use a reference data architecture as your starting point.

A reference data architecture is a high-level blueprint that guides the design and implementation of data solutions. It defines the principles, guidelines, and standards for collecting, storing, integrating, and delivering data as products. Think of it as a reusable map: rather than starting from a blank page, solution architects and teams can use the reference architecture as a menu of proven building blocks, and then customize for their specific needs.

The benefit of working this way is threefold. First, it accelerates delivery by allowing teams to reuse existing patterns rather than creating bespoke designs from scratch. Second, it improves quality and reduces risk because security, reliability, and governance requirements can be embedded in blueprints and reused systematically. Third, over time, this also rationalizes the technology stack, avoids unnecessary tool sprawl, and strengthens vendor relationships by making clear which core platforms will be widely adopted.

Figure 11 below shows a reference architecture framework for data products. It depicts the end-to-end flow, from data sources on the left, through management, processing, and enrichment, into data products, and finally out to consumers and use cases. Let's walk through the main components from left to right:

- **Data Sources**: Inputs to data products, coming from internal systems like ERP, CRM, or transaction platforms, as well as external and third-party providers.

- **Data Ingestion**: Mechanisms to bring data into the platform, unaltered, at the required frequency and format.

- **Data Products**: Raw data first lands as-is, then is curated and quality-controlled, enriched with transformations or features, and finally packaged as consumable products.

- **Data Management**: Capabilities such as metadata management, data quality, and cataloging provide governance, consistency, and transparency throughout the flow.

- **Processing and Storage**: Orchestration, compute, storage, and staging environments support the heavy lifting of transforming and preparing data.

- **Data Science**: For certain products, analytics or AI layers are added to curated data to generate predictive or prescriptive insights.

- **Consumption**: The final stage where data products are delivered into reports, dashboards, APIs, queries, or directly into business workflows and AI models.

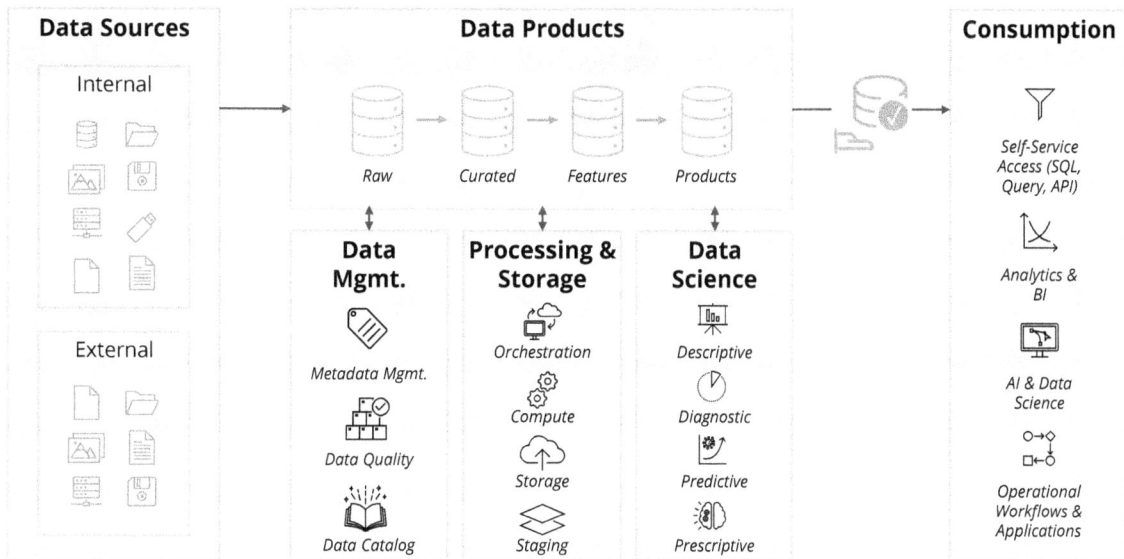

Figure 11 – A reference data architecture for Data Products.

This framework provides a shared vocabulary and a consistent starting point for any team embarking on the design of a new data product. In the next part of this section, we will show how organizations can go one step further by mapping specific technologies or tools onto each component, creating actionable blueprints that guide implementation.

Now that we have outlined the general reference architecture for data products, the next step is to make it concrete within a specific technology environment. Figure 12 shows how this architecture can be realized natively in AWS.

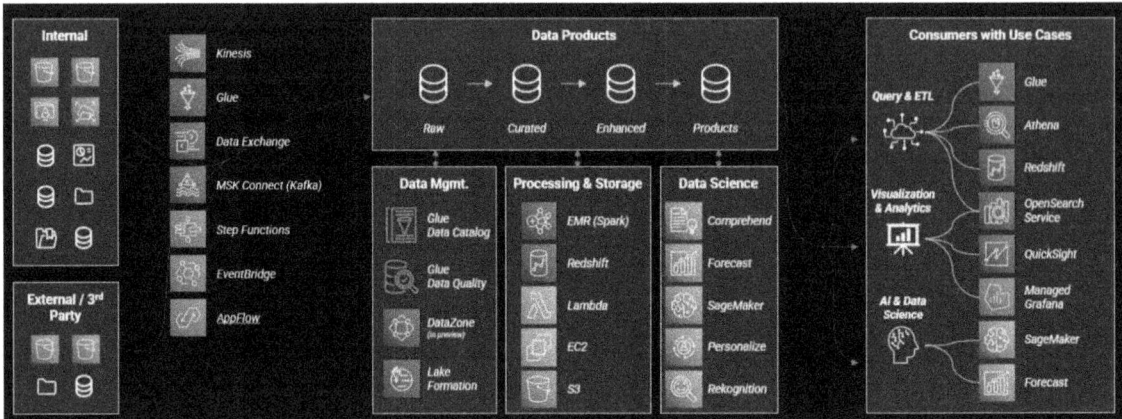

Figure 12 – Reference data architecture for Data Products fully provisioned on AWS. Retrieved from (Koenders, A simple reference architecture for data products, 2023).

By mapping each component to AWS-managed services, teams can more easily decide which tools to use and how to assemble them into a working product:

- **Data sources:** S3 and File Caches are common options to complement existing data sources. For organizations already building out a data lake, Data Lake for AWS provides a more flexible set of storage options.

- **Data ingestion:** AWS offers a broad set of ingestion services. Kinesis can be used for streaming data, Glue for ETL jobs, and Data Exchange for integrating external and third-party datasets. MSK Connect brings in data from Apache Kafka clusters. Step Functions can orchestrate serverless integration workflows, while EventBridge handles event-driven data pushes. AppFlow provides out-of-the-box connectivity with SaaS applications such as SAP and Salesforce.

- **Data management:** Glue Data Catalog and DataZone are central to discovering, cataloging, and advertising data products while managing metadata. Glue Data Quality provides capabilities for measuring and monitoring quality, while Lake Formation supports secure access control and data provisioning across the environment.

- **Data processing and storage:** EMR and Redshift are strong options for data warehousing solutions if the data product requires them. Lambda provides serverless, event-driven compute, while EC2 and S3 can be configured and managed more directly for broader storage and processing needs.

- **Data science:** AWS provides a comprehensive suite of services across the data science lifecycle. Comprehend applies natural language processing to analyze and extract insights from text. Forecast can generate demand or business forecasts. SageMaker provides a platform for building, training, and deploying machine learning models. Personalize enables real-time user recommendations. Rekognition analyzes images and videos for object detection, facial analysis, and text extraction.

- **Data distribution:** For query and ETL, Glue, Athena, and Redshift provide multiple access patterns. QuickSight can be used for basic visualization, and OpenSearch supports more advanced search and ingestion requirements. On the consuming side, AWS AI and analytics services such as SageMaker, Forecast, and others can connect directly to hosted data products to power downstream use cases.

As you can see, once provided with this kind of reference architecture, the task of designing and building a data product becomes far more straightforward. It shifts from starting with a blank sheet to focusing on the specific business and technical requirements, and then matching them with the right AWS services.

Similar views can be built for Microsoft Azure, Google Cloud Platform, Snowflake, or hybrid stacks. In practice, many organizations also combine AWS with other platforms for specialized needs. For example, one company I worked with ran its data products on AWS, but integrated Informatica for data cataloging and ETL, and MuleSoft for API management.

2.3.2. Architecture Guidelines

In a previous section, we walked through the end-to-end lifecycle of data products. Now, if we zoom in on that lifecycle, one part that quickly stands out as especially important is having architectural standards in place. These standards serve as a set of rules or blueprints that guide the design, development, and maintenance of data products.

Why does this matter? Getting things right at the very beginning, during ideation and design, prevents a lot of problems later on. When data products are created consistently and well-structured, they are easier to trust and reuse and less likely to create technical debt or chaos in the long run. Architectural standards also mean that best practices are embedded from the start, rather than bolted on as an afterthought. That leads to faster adoption, fewer surprises, and a more scalable data ecosystem. Another reason standards are so valuable is that they allow for consistency across teams and across time. If every team builds its data products differently, the result is confusion and duplication. But when there's a clear set of guidelines, people know what to expect and can more easily combine or connect products. It also helps with governance, because standards make it easier to attach controls and measure compliance.

So, what do we actually mean when we talk about architectural standards for data products? Think of it like the construction industry. You would never want buildings to be designed and built completely independently, without common codes or shared principles. If that happened, buildings might be unsafe, every project would reinvent the proverbial wheel, and there would be no way to ensure they work together as part of a neighborhood. The same goes for data products. Without standards, each one might "stand up" on its own, but together they would be fragile, inconsistent, and hard to use. With that in mind, let's look at five specific categories of architectural guidelines:

- **Product Specification**: Defines what a data product is and what it contains. This covers its boundaries, ownership, and canonical dataset. It ensures each product is independent, atomic, and well-described.

- **Coding and Automation**: Captures everything "as code," from data pipelines and infrastructure to access rules, making products repeatable, testable, and scalable.

- **Metadata and Observability**: Focuses on ensuring that products are well documented, traceable, and continuously monitored for quality and performance.

- **Data Quality and Integrity**: Embeds controls, validation, and testing so that trust in the data is built by design, not by inspection.

- **Data Access and Sharing**: Ensures products can be safely and easily used by others, with clear access controls, sharing mechanisms, and governance baked in.

Product Specification	Coding & Automation	Metadata & Observability	Data Quality & Integrity	Data Access & Sharing
Boundaries	Infrastructure-as-Code	Lineage	Validation	RBAC / Least Privilege
Ownership	Pipelines-as-Code	Documentation	Completeness	Secure Sharing
Canonical Dataset	CI/CD	SLAs	Consistency	Data Contracts
Atomic	Automation	Freshness	Testing	APIs / Views
Declarative Spec	Repeatability	Anomalies	Monitoring	Governance

Figure 13 – Five categories of architecture guidelines for data product design.

2.3.2.1. Product Specification Guidelines

When we talk about architecture guidelines for data products, a natural starting point is how the product itself is defined. Before you think about pipelines, tools, or governance, you need to be clear on what the product is. Product specification and structure guidelines provide that foundation. They define the boundaries, scope, and formal description of a data product so that it can stand on its own, be trusted by consumers, and be managed consistently.

Why does this matter? If you don't establish strong product definitions, data assets can quickly turn into scattered datasets, partial solutions, or fragile links between systems. That makes them harder to use and harder to govern. By contrast, well-specified products are reusable, auditable, and easier to maintain. They also allow teams across the organization to speak the same language, because everyone knows what each data product is and how to access it.

A key principle here is that a data product should be an independent, atomic unit. Independent means that it can function on its own without being deeply entangled with other systems. Atomic means it is the smallest meaningful unit of value. It is complete enough to be useful, but not so large as to bundle unrelated datasets. And unit means it is treated as a product in its own right: cataloged, owned, and consumed as a single entity. This independence is what makes products easier to govern and evolve.

Another important guideline is to use a declarative product specification. Instead of informal descriptions hidden in documentation or email, every product should be formally defined in a structured template or specification language. This spells out inputs, outputs, transformation logic, ownership, and policies. It ensures that products are transparent, consistent, and portable.

Finally, each data product should ideally expose a single canonical dataset, which is a denormalized version of the truth that all consumers can rely on. Exposing multiple versions of the same data creates confusion and undermines trust. By enforcing a single canonical output (even if exposed through multiple ports, such as SQL tables or APIs), you provide clarity and reduce duplication.

Together, these guidelines ensure that, from day one, every data product is clearly scoped, consistently defined, and consumable as a trusted unit. They prevent confusion and lay the foundation for scale across the rest of the lifecycle.

2.3.2.2. Coding and Automation

The second set of architecture guidelines for data products is about coding everything you can. This includes pipelines, infrastructure, permissions, and even the rules governing how products are used. In modern data environments, this approach is often described as "as-code". Examples include infrastructure-as-code, access-policies-as-code, or pipelines-as-code. The idea is that every step in building, deploying, and running a data product is written down in code so it can be repeated, tested, and automated.

This matters because it removes manual, error-prone work. Instead of someone configuring servers, permissions, or pipelines by hand, everything is defined once in code and then applied consistently across environments. That means fewer mistakes, faster changes, and a system that is much easier to maintain and scale. For data products, which are often reused by many teams and need to run reliably every day, this is critical.

Key guidelines in this category include coding ingestion and publishing steps to ensure data always moves in a predictable way, and using infrastructure-as-code to automatically provision storage, compute, and monitoring. Access rules should also be defined as code—permissions, user roles, and policies become part of the product itself rather than separate documentation. CI/CD pipelines should handle building, testing, and deploying new changes so updates happen quickly and safely. Metadata collection (also see the next set of guidelines) can also be automated as part of these pipelines, ensuring that definitions and freshness are always kept up to date.

Taken together, coding and automation ensure that data assets can be stood up in new environments, updated without downtime, and scaled without introducing risk because the rules of how they work are captured in code.

2.3.2.3. Metadata and Observability

Metadata is what makes data products understandable, traceable, and reusable. Without it, even the best-engineered products quickly become black boxes that nobody trusts or can confidently use. Strong metadata practices ensure every data product clearly communicates what it is, who owns it, how it's structured, and how it should be consumed.

Metadata turns raw information into usable, governable data.

Architecturally, metadata guidelines focus on consistency, visibility, and interoperability. Every product should be registered in an enterprise catalog that provides a shared taxonomy and a single source of truth for discovery. Always document core information like ownership, purpose, schema, SLAs, lineage, refresh cadence, and quality indicators. Metadata also needs to show how the product is distributed, what formats or APIs expose it, and must track deprecations or breaking changes over time.

Good metadata design also supports governance and collaboration. Access requirements, approvals, and usage policies can be embedded directly into the metadata, not scattered across emails or documents. Similarly, metadata should make data quality transparent, showing health status and SLA adherence at a glance.

To make metadata actionable, it should be easily searchable, written in plain language, and enriched with practical examples, such as sample queries or notebooks, to help users get started. Finally, observability is key: to the extent possible, data products should automatically track lineage, freshness, drift, and anomalies so that users always know whether the data is current and reliable.

When applied to our Finance Reconciliation Engine, these principles mean that the product appears in the enterprise catalog with clear ownership, quality metrics, and distribution details. Users can see where the data originates, how it flows through the system, and whether it meets agreed accuracy and timeliness standards.

2.3.2.4. Data Quality and Integrity

Data quality and integrity are what make a data product trustworthy. Without them, no amount of architecture or engineering can make people actually rely on the data. This category of architectural guidelines focuses on designing quality directly into the product rather than trying to fix issues after the fact. Good data products should be self-checking, transparent about their health, and proactive in preventing bad data from spreading downstream.

Quality starts in the pipelines. Reliability and integrity rules, such as freshness, completeness, and referential consistency, should be embedded directly into data processing steps. Every transformation should include automated checks to validate that results are correct. When something goes wrong, such as a delayed feed or a schema change, automated alerts must warn the right people immediately. Continuous monitoring ensures issues are caught early, not discovered during audits or reports.

Visibility is another cornerstone. A strong data product publishes its quality status and service level agreements (SLAs) in the metadata catalog so users can see at a glance how accurate and fresh the data is. If there are known issues or temporary exceptions, those should be documented openly. This transparency builds trust, and trust drives adoption.

Finally, testing matters. Automated unit tests are a key defense against data drift and broken logic because they make sure that what you think is happening in your pipelines actually is. Together, these practices ensure that a data product is not just built once and forgotten but remains reliable and accurate throughout its lifecycle.

For the Finance Reconciliation Engine, this means validation steps that reject records without transaction IDs, daily checks confirming a 99% match rate, and SLA commitments such as "daily refresh, over 98 percent accuracy." The system triggers alerts when a bank feed is delayed, and all results are visible through a catalog "green light" status that indicates users can trust the output.

2.3.2.5. Usage and Access

Data sharing and access are what make a data product usable in practice.

Even the best-built data product has no value if people cannot find it, connect to it, or use it safely.

This set of architectural guidelines aims to make data easy to access and reuse while keeping it secure and well-controlled. It ensures that teams can share data confidently without creating risk or unnecessary complexity. A key principle is to avoid creating extra copies of data. Instead of exporting files all over the place, data products should make their information available through virtual views or APIs that others can query directly. When sharing data within the same platform, use built-in secure-share features. If a copy is really needed, it should still follow the same governance, encryption, and access rules.

Access should never be a free-for-all. Approvals, logging, and the ability to remove access are all essential. Every interface, such as an API or SQL view, should have a clear version and contract so that consumers know how to use it and what to expect when it changes. Data contracts should spell out the schema, definitions, and update policies so that no one is surprised later.

Teams also need to make sure their data can connect with others. Using common identifiers and shared dimensions makes it easy to combine datasets. Finally, all access should follow the least-privilege principle: people get only what they need, and everything is logged for visibility and audit. For example, in the Finance Reconciliation Engine, the reconciled transactions are shared directly through Redshift views rather than exported to CSV files. The audit team accesses the data through a secure Redshift share, and any API access requires an IAM approval workflow. The schemas are versioned and follow a clear contract stating that "amount" is always stored in USD, and every access event is logged in CloudTrail. This keeps sharing simple, consistent, and secure.

2.3.3. Regulatory, Privacy, and Compliance Guidelines

As data products increasingly power critical business decisions and customer-facing experiences, they also inherit the regulatory and compliance responsibilities of the data they process. This section outlines the key frameworks, laws, and standards that shape how data products must be designed, governed, and operated to remain compliant. While the specific obligations vary by industry and geography, the underlying goal is the same: to protect data integrity, ensure privacy, and maintain trust in the systems that use it.

To make sense of this landscape, we'll group the most relevant guidelines into four categories that together provide a practical foundation for compliance by design. Figure 14 below presents these four categories, with example frameworks listed for each.

Compliance Frameworks			
Information Security & Privacy Management	**IT Governance, Quality & Service Management**	**Sector-Specific / Regulated-Domain Standards**	**Data Ethics & Responsible AI**
ISO 27001	COBIT	FDA 21 CFR Part 11	EU AI Act
SOC 2	ISO/IEC 38500	ISO 13485	OECD Principles on AI
GDPR	ISO 8000	HIPAA	UNESCO AI Ethics
CCPA	ITIL	PCI DSS	NIST AI RMF
HIPAA	ISO/IEC 20000	GLBA	FAT Principles
NIST Cybersecurity		Basel III / BCBS 239	

Figure 14 – A set of the most common and important compliance frameworks for data products.

2.3.3.1. Information Security and Privacy Management

Information security and privacy management are about keeping data safe and using it responsibly. Every data product must protect the information it handles and ensure it's used only for the right reasons. This includes preventing unauthorized access, loss, or misuse, as well as ensuring compliance with privacy laws such as GDPR and HIPAA.

For data product teams, this means embedding protection into the design from the start, not adding it later. Access should be limited to those who need it, sensitive fields should be encrypted, and activities should be logged and monitored. Privacy considerations, such as collecting only what's needed, masking personal identifiers, and defining retention rules, should be built into pipelines and storage layers.

Key standards and frameworks commonly used include the following:

- **ISO 27001**: Sets requirements for an Information Security Management System (ISMS) covering risk management, access control, encryption, and incident response.

- **SOC two (Service Organization Controls Type 2)**: Focuses on trust principles such as security, availability, processing integrity, confidentiality, and privacy for service providers.

- **GDPR (General Data Protection Regulation)**: Defines rules for the collection, processing, and sharing of personal data, emphasizing consent and user rights.

- **CCPA (California Consumer Privacy Act)**: Similar to GDPR, it gives consumers the right to know, delete, and control how their data is used.

- **HIPAA (Health Insurance Portability and Accountability Act)**: Protects personal health information in healthcare and related systems.

- **NIST Cybersecurity Framework**: Provides guidelines for identifying, protecting, detecting, responding to, and recovering from cybersecurity threats.

2.3.3.2. IT Governance, Quality, and Service Management

IT governance, quality, and service management are about making sure that data products are managed with the same discipline and reliability as any other core business system. It's about ensuring it continues to perform, stays aligned with business priorities, and follows clear processes for maintenance, change, and improvement.

This means defining who is accountable for what, tracking performance and quality, and following structured ways of managing changes, risks, and incidents. For data product teams, it also means having clear release processes, version control, testing procedures, and service-level expectations. Good governance ensures consistency and trust in how data products are delivered and maintained across teams and environments. Key standards and frameworks commonly used include the following:

- **COBIT (Control Objectives for Information and Related Technologies)**: Provides a governance framework for aligning IT activities with business goals, managing risk, and ensuring accountability.

- **ISO/IEC 38500**: Offers guiding principles for effective IT governance, focusing on responsibility, strategy, acquisition, performance, conformance, and human behavior.

- **ISO 8000**: Focuses on data quality management, defining how data should be measured, validated, and maintained to remain accurate and reliable.

- **ITIL (Information Technology Infrastructure Library)**: Outlines best practices for IT service management, including incident response, problem management, and continuous improvement.

- **ISO/IEC 20000**: Sets requirements for service management systems, ensuring consistent delivery of high-quality IT and data services.

2.2.3.3. Sector-Specific or Regulated-Domain Standards

Different industries have their own rules for handling, storing, and sharing data. These sector-specific standards exist because the risks and sensitivities of data vary. Financial data, patient records, or medical device information each require a different level of control and traceability. For data product teams, this means understanding which regulations apply to their business and designing products that meet those requirements from day one.

In practice, this can affect how data is collected, validated, stored, and even displayed. It might mean adding audit trails for every data change, controlling access to sensitive fields, or verifying that digital systems can be trusted to produce accurate, traceable records. These rules often come with documentation and validation expectations, where compliance is also about evidence and process discipline. Common industry-specific frameworks and standards include:

- **FDA 21 CFR Part 11**: Defines how electronic records and electronic signatures must be managed for compliance in life sciences and medical devices.

- **ISO 13485**: Sets quality management requirements for medical device manufacturing and related software.

- **HIPAA (Health Insurance Portability and Accountability Act)**: Protects health information and governs how it can be used and disclosed in healthcare.

- **PCI DSS (Payment Card Industry Data Security Standard)**: Governs how credit card data must be stored, processed, and transmitted securely.

- **GLBA (Gramm-Leach-Bliley Act)**: Requires financial institutions to explain their information-sharing practices and safeguard sensitive customer data.

- **Basel III/BCBS 239**: Establishes data aggregation and reporting principles for banks and financial institutions.

2.3.3.4. Data Ethics and Responsible AI

Data ethics and responsible AI are about using data and algorithms in ways that are fair, transparent, and accountable. As organizations rely more on automated systems and AI models, it's not enough for data products to simply be accurate or compliant—they must also respect people's rights, avoid bias, and make decisions that can be explained and justified. For data product teams, this means thinking beyond technical performance and considering social impact. Teams should ask questions like: Is this data used in a way the user would expect? Could this model unfairly disadvantage a group of people? Are the results explainable to both experts and non-experts? Responsible design requires visibility into how data is sourced, how models are trained, and how outcomes are monitored over time. Key frameworks and principles commonly referenced:

- **EU AI Act**: Introduces risk-based rules for AI systems, emphasizing transparency, human oversight, and accountability.

- **OECD Principles on AI**: Promote fairness, safety, transparency, and accountability in AI systems.

- **UNESCO Recommendation on the Ethics of AI**: Guides governments and organizations on ethical AI use worldwide.

- **NIST AI Risk Management Framework (AI RMF)**: Helps identify, measure, and manage risks in AI development and deployment.

- **Fairness, Accountability, and Transparency (FAT) Principles**: A widely used set of practical guidelines for building responsible AI systems.

- **Company Codes of Ethics**: Many organizations create internal policies or "AI charters" that define how data and algorithms should be used responsibly.

2.3.4. Certification of Data Products

This section introduces a clear and practical way to ensure that every data product meets a consistent baseline before it is released for broader use. It builds directly on the previous sections: the reference data architecture, the architectural guidelines, and the regulatory, privacy, and compliance expectations. Certification brings these elements together and turns them into a unified, easy-to-apply set of standards that any team can follow. We'll outline the certification standards, why they matter, and how they help teams deliver data products that are safe, reliable, and compliant by design.

2.3.4.1. Certification Standards

While these frameworks and principles across ethics, AI, privacy, security, and governance look different on paper, they are not separate worlds. In practice, they overlap heavily. If every data product owner had to fully understand the EU AI Act, GDPR, ISO 27001, and ITIL in detail, they'd never get any work done. The key is recognizing that most of these frameworks share the same foundation.

When you translate all these regulations and standards into what they actually mean for a data product, you end up with a smaller, unified set of common-sense practices that apply almost everywhere. These are the practical habits that make a data product safe, compliant, and trustworthy, regardless of which specific regulation or audit you're dealing with. For example, take traceability and accountability:

- Under **ISO 27001**, it means logging who accessed what data and when.
- Under **GDPR**, it means being able to show how personal data is processed and by whom.
- Under **the EU AI Act**, this means understanding how an algorithm arrived at its decision.
- Under **COBIT or ITIL**, it means maintaining an audit trail for every change or release.

The form may differ, but the spirit is the same: be able to explain what happened, why, and who or what was responsible.

Or let's take another example, this time about clear and consistent definitions of the data product and of the data attributes inside it:

- Under **ISO 8000 (Data Quality)**, this is about ensuring that every data element has an agreed, unambiguous meaning. Each attribute, like "customer ID" or "transaction date", must be defined, validated, and used consistently across systems.

- Under **GDPR (Privacy)**, this matters because you must be able to identify exactly which fields represent personal data, how they are processed, and for what purpose. If "email" or "user ID" isn't clearly defined, you can't manage consent or erasure properly.

- Under **FDA 21 CFR Part 11 (Life Sciences)**, clear definitions ensure that data used in electronic records or reports can be trusted and reproduced. Every field in a regulated dataset must be traceable to a controlled definition so that results are scientifically and legally valid.

Different frameworks might describe this in their own language (e.g., concepts such as "metadata," "data dictionary," or "controlled terminology"). Still, the underlying principle is the same: you are expected to know what each piece of data means.

Compliance across frameworks can be simplified into a small number of shared design principles that every data product can follow.
These principles form the backbone of "compliance by design."

Such principles and standards can form the foundation for data product certification. Here, certification does not necessarily mean issuing a formal certificate. Instead, it means holding each data product and its owner accountable for meeting a clear baseline before the product is considered ready for broader use. Table 11 illustrates an example of such a set of minimally required certification standards.

These certification standards are not meant to be rigid checklists that every data product must implement in exactly the same way. What matters most is that each team thinks deliberately about how these dimensions apply and makes conscious decisions. If data product teams across the organization approach these dimensions in a broadly consistent way, it becomes much easier to govern and scale.

Dimension	Standard Summary
🧑 Ownership	The data product must have a designated owner accountable for its value, quality, and long-term stewardship.
🗃 Catalog and Metadata	The data product must be registered in the catalog with complete, accurate, and consistently maintained metadata.
🔐 Security	The data product must enforce least-privilege access, encryption, and monitoring aligned to its data classification.
🔗 Interoperability	The data product must use shared identifiers, structures, and conventions to ensure consistent cross-domain integration.
📑 Retention and Disposal	The data product must follow defined retention schedules and implement secure, auditable disposal procedures.
💾 Backup and Recovery	The data product must maintain a tested backup and recovery process to ensure continuity and resilience.
✔ Quality and Reliability	The data product must implement embedded validation controls to maintain accuracy, completeness, and consistent performance.
🚨 Incident Response	The data product must have a defined process for issue detection, escalation, and timely resolution.
📝 Documentation	The data product must include clear, current documentation covering design, logic, dependencies, and operations.
📊 Adoption and Impact	The data product must track usage and measure business outcomes to validate continued relevance and value.

Table 11 – A set of data product certification criteria.

For example, if every team maintains its own disconnected metadata process, you end up with chaos. But if all teams register their products in a shared data catalog and follow a streamlined, perhaps automated, process for publishing metadata, it saves enormous time and enables transparency across the entire data ecosystem. Let's consider the 10 data product certification criteria shown in Table 11:

- **Ownership:** Every data product must have a single owner. Someone who stands up and takes responsibility for the business value, quality, and long-term purpose. This owner is not just a technical steward. It is the person who ensures that the product continues to justify its existence. Data owners understand their users, can explain and defend why it matters, and ensure it evolves as needs change. A strong owner treats the data product as a living asset, always verifying that it remains fit for purpose, aligned with policy, and actively delivering value. For a broader discussion of roles and responsibilities, see the next chapter on Data Product Teams and Governance.

- **Catalog and Metadata:** If your organization has a data catalog or data marketplace, every data product should be registered there. If such a catalog does not exist, each product should at least maintain a minimal metadata record describing its purpose, source systems, data model, refresh frequency, and owner. This record forms the product's identity. Among the more critical metadata fields is data classification, which is the label that tells you whether the product contains public, internal, confidential, or restricted data. Classification guides how information must be protected, shared, and retained. The more consistent the metadata is across data products, the easier it becomes to search, connect, and govern them collectively.

- **Security:** Security covers how data products control access, protect sensitive content, and monitor use. Access should always follow the principle of least privilege, where users only get what they need for approved use cases. Authentication and authorization rules must match the data's classification level, with stronger protections for restricted data. Data should be encrypted both at rest and in transit, ensuring confidentiality and integrity even if systems are compromised. Access logs and monitoring should capture who accessed the data product, when, and (although this might be a bit harder at times) for what purpose.

- **Interoperability:** A good data product doesn't live in isolation. It connects with other products and systems through shared standards, consistent identifiers, and aligned semantics. Interoperability ensures that data can flow smoothly across domains without repeated transformation or manual work. Interoperability increases as more common structures, reference data, and naming conventions are used. Bringing in interoperability standards is one of the most effective ways to make sure this happens consistently across data products. These standards define how products should be connected, described, and exchanged, making integration simpler and more predictable. A shared semantic layer, with common business definitions and metrics, helps everyone interpret data the same way, reducing duplication and confusion. Likewise, maintaining a rationalized set of integration tools (for example, a standard approach for batch, API, or streaming connections) makes it easier for teams to connect systems securely and efficiently.

- **Retention and Disposal:** Every data product should have a retention schedule: a clear policy defining how long its data should be kept and when it should be deleted. Retention schedules reduce legal and privacy risks, control storage costs, and maintain focus on data that is actually needed. In practice, this often means setting different retention periods based on data classification. Disposal should be deliberate and auditable, ensuring that data is securely erased when its purpose has expired.

- **Backup and Recovery:** Data products must be resilient to failure. Having a reliable, tested backup and recovery process means that, if something goes wrong (e.g., a system crash, accidental deletion, or data corruption), you can restore the product quickly without losing trust or availability. The best teams test these processes regularly rather than waiting for an emergency.

- **Quality and Reliability:** For a data product to be truly used in important business processes, it must first be trusted. People rely on a data product for critical decisions only when they are confident that the numbers and outputs it produces are accurate. That trust comes from deliberate attention to quality and reliability. This does not mean that every data product needs a full-blown data quality dashboard or complex metric calculations. What matters is that teams think about quality deliberately and apply the right controls for their specific product. In some cases, that might mean setting up reconciliation checks to confirm that totals or records match across systems. In others, it could mean locking down data pipelines so that only valid formats or approved values can pass through. Automated data validation rules are another good practice, catching problems before they reach consumers.

- **Incident Response:** No matter how well a data product is built, things can still go wrong. Pipelines fail, data loads stop, or numbers look off. When that happens, users shouldn't be left wondering what to do or who to contact. Just like any other product, whether it's a pair of shoes, a TV, or an internet service, people expect that if something isn't working as it should, there's someone to turn to who will help fix it. A good incident response setup makes sure there's always a clear path for users to raise issues and for someone to respond. It doesn't need to be a formal "support center," but it should be clear who owns the problem and how it gets resolved. The goal isn't to eliminate every issue, but to ensure that when issues do occur, they're noticed, owned, and handled. Having that simple level of responsiveness builds trust and keeps the data product usable.

- **Documentation:** Comprehensive and current documentation is the backbone of maintainability. It explains how the data product is built, how it works, and how to troubleshoot or extend it. Good documentation reduces reliance on individual expertise, simplifies onboarding new team members, and provides the transparency needed for audits or reviews. It's also how you fight the ancient old enemy of every data organization: tribal knowledge. Tribal knowledge is when only a few people know how things work, and progress stops when they're unavailable. Clear, well-maintained documentation keeps that knowledge in the open, making it easier for others to step in, learn, and contribute. The best teams treat documentation as part of the product itself, not an afterthought.

- **Adoption and Impact:** Finally, every data product should link back to the use cases it serves and the outcomes it enables. Tracking adoption helps verify its business relevance. Measuring impact in terms of saved time, improved decisions, or reduced risk allows teams to prioritize investment where it truly matters. A data product that is not used or does not deliver measurable value should be reviewed or retired.

Let's return to our example, the Finance Reconciliation Engine, to see what these certification standards look like in real life. Table 12 shows a practical implementation of each standard, including the kinds of tools, controls, and processes a real data product team uses to meet them. Now, let's take the specifications we have for the Finance Reconciliation Engine and confirm the original hypothesis. By following a simple, rationalized set of certification standards, you can naturally meet the broader range of regulatory and compliance requirements that apply to this kind of data product. In other words, if the data product is designed and operated according to these standards, it should meet many (or all) of the same expectations that formal frameworks and audits seek. For instance, the Sarbanes-Oxley Act (SOX) requires financial reporting systems to maintain data integrity, accuracy, and traceability for audit purposes. In the reconciliation engine, the combination of Ownership, Catalog, and Metadata, and Quality and Reliability standards covers this. The data owner defined in the catalog provides accountability, metadata captures lineage and change history, and automated reconciliation checks ensure accuracy between ERP, payment, and bank systems. Together, these practices deliver full SOX alignment without any additional manual controls.

Certification Standard	Illustration: Finance Reconciliation Engine
Ownership	The Finance Data Product Owner owns the Finance Reconciliation Engine within the FP&A (Financial Planning and Analysis) department. They review monthly reconciliation accuracy reports, approve schema or logic changes, and ensure that reconciled totals match general ledger entries in SAP S/4HANA. Ownership is logged in the data catalog with name, title, and escalation contact.
Catalog and Metadata	The data product is registered in the Informatica Data Catalog and synced automatically from Snowflake. Metadata includes schema, lineage, refresh schedule, data source (e.g., SAP, Stripe, and Bank of America feeds), and business owner. Classification tags mark tables containing sensitive financial and PII data. Each table and column is documented with business definitions and data types.
Security	Access is managed through Okta using role-based access control (RBAC) in Snowflake. Finance Analysts have read-only access, while Data Engineers have restricted write access to transformation logic in dbt. All data in Snowflake is encrypted at rest (AES-256) and in transit (TLS 1.2). Access logs are stored in Splunk for monitoring and auditing.
Interoperability Standards	The reconciliation engine publishes a canonical output table called FIN_RECON_SUMMARY_V1 accessible via Snowflake's Secure Data Share and a REST API built in AWS API Gateway. It follows standard naming conventions (DOMAIN_ENTITY_METRIC_VERSION) and exposes definitions through the semantic layer in dbt. Batch data loads are handled via Airflow DAGs, while real-time exception alerts are sent through Kafka topics.
Retention and Disposal	Source-level transaction data is retained for seven years to meet SOX audit requirements, while intermediate reconciliation logs are kept for 90 days. A retention policy in Snowflake automatically drops old tables using lifecycle scripts triggered by Terraform. Disposal logs are archived in AWS S3 Glacier for recordkeeping.
Backup and Recovery	Daily backups of Snowflake databases are managed through Time Travel (7-day recovery window) and periodic snapshot exports to AWS S3. A disaster recovery plan allows the system to be redeployed in AWS us-west-2 using Terraform templates within four hours of an outage.
Quality and Reliability	Data quality rules are defined in Great Expectations and integrated into the Airflow pipeline. Key checks include record count reconciliation between SAP and Stripe, validation of currency formats (USD, EUR), and duplicate transaction detection. Failures trigger Slack alerts to the finance data team. A daily reconciliation score is logged in the catalog.
Incident Response	When reconciliation jobs fail, alerts are automatically sent via PagerDuty to the on-call data engineer. Users can raise incidents through a ServiceNow form tagged under "Finance Data Products." A resolution SLA of four business hours applies to critical incidents. Incident logs and root-cause analyses are tracked in Confluence.
Documentation	All pipeline logic, transformations, and data model diagrams are stored in Confluence, linked directly from the data catalog. Each dbt model includes an auto-generated docstring describing its purpose and inputs. A "Runbook" explains how to refresh, test, and troubleshoot the engine, helping new engineers onboard quickly and reducing reliance on tribal knowledge.
Adoption and Impact	The engine's usage is tracked through Snowflake query logs and a dashboard in Tableau that shows monthly active users and reconciliation accuracy rates. Since go-live, it has reduced manual reconciliation effort by 85% and shortened month-end close by two days. These impact metrics are reviewed quarterly by the Finance Steering Committee.

Table 12 – Practical illustration of how data certification standards are implemented for the Financial Reconciliation Engine data product.

Another example is ISO 27001, which sets expectations around information security management. The Security standard, with encryption at rest and in transit, role-based access through Okta, and activity logging in Splunk, directly maps to ISO 27001 Annex A controls (especially those related to access management, encryption, and monitoring). Because these controls are part of the certification process itself, the data product automatically meets ISO security requirements without separate compliance projects.

Finally, consider the GDPR, which requires clear definitions and the protection of personal data. Through the Catalog and Metadata standard, every data field is classified, including those with personal identifiers such as customer IDs or payment references. The Retention and Disposal policy enforces data minimization and ensures that records are deleted once their business purpose has ended. This satisfies GDPR principles of purpose limitation and storage limitation, baked directly into how the product operates.

These examples show how a lean set of certification standards can serve as a practical bridge between data product design and compliance. Instead of managing dozens of external frameworks separately, teams can follow one consistent approach, and compliance largely takes care of itself.

2.3.4.2. Why Certification Standards Matter in Practice

In the previous section, we explored what certification standards are and how they help teams design and operate strong, trustworthy data products. We also looked at a concrete example through the Finance Reconciliation Engine, showing how these standards come to life in practice. But before moving on, it's worth reflecting on what makes these standards powerful and how to use them without turning them into bureaucracy.

The goal here isn't to make data teams fill out endless checklists. It's to ensure that every team deliberately considers what makes their data product dependable, secure, and valuable. The word *product* in data product matters. It implies that there are users, and that those users will keep coming back only if they can trust it, understand it, and connect to it easily. A product mindset means designing with adoption, usability, and reliability in mind.

When applied well, certification standards become guardrails rather than gates. They help ensure that all the basics are handled consistently, so each data product team doesn't have to rediscover them from scratch. In other words, by embedding these standards into the design process, compliance and governance almost take care of themselves. Teams can focus on building value while knowing they're already aligned with regulatory and enterprise expectations.

I have personally seen across a series of organizations, both mid-size companies as well as corporations that are leading their respective sectors, that this approach has proven to be one of the great simplifiers of data governance. It enables consistent management of critical data assets across teams, domains, and tools. When certification standards are tied directly to shared platforms, such as a data catalog, a quality monitoring tool, or a metadata-driven integration framework, you start seeing the real benefits. Governance becomes automated, onboarding gets faster, and good practices spread naturally through the organization.

Finally, it's important to connect these certification standards back to the data product lifecycle we defined earlier in this chapter. These criteria should not be seen as an extra set of steps on top of the lifecycle. In fact, if you follow the lifecycle properly, from ideation to design, build, validation, and ongoing operation, you already address these standards by design. The lifecycle itself ensures that ownership, metadata, quality, and governance are built in from the start.

However, having an explicit list of certification criteria still makes a big difference during the design and build stages. It gives data product teams a clear, concrete reference to verify compliance and helps them easily incorporate best practices without having to interpret policies or frameworks on their own. In short, the lifecycle provides the flow, and certification standards provide the checkpoints, together creating a simple, repeatable way to deliver strong, compliant, and trusted data products.

CHAPTER 3

People and Change

In the first chapter, we laid the foundation for what data products are, including their defining characteristics, guiding principles, and why they represent a better way to manage and deliver data. In the second chapter, we put those ideas into practice by exploring how great data products are designed and built, from lifecycle and business case development to architectural blueprints and certification criteria.

Now, in this final part of the book, we'll turn to the human side of data products: the people and the change it takes to make them successful. Technology and architecture can provide the structure, but it's people, collaboration, and culture that determine whether data products truly deliver value. We'll explore this across four dimensions:

1. **Data Product Teams**: What good data product teams look like, the roles and responsibilities that make them effective, and how they work together.

2. **Data Product Portfolios**: How organizations move beyond individual products to manage a cohesive, balanced portfolio of data products that align with strategic priorities.

3. **Maturity Models and Change Enablement**: How teams evolve their practices, drive adoption, and create lasting behavioral change so that data products are used, trusted, and continuously improved.

4. **The Organizational Change Journey**: What it takes to transform into a data product–driven organization, including common phases, success factors, and pitfalls to avoid.

3.1. Data Product Teams, Roles, and Responsibilities

Imagine you're a chef. Before you serve a meal, you gather ingredients from different places, make sure they're fresh and safe to eat, and then combine them in a way that brings out the right flavors for the people you expect to serve. A data product is very similar. It's made up of data collected for a specific purpose. But before that data can be "served," it needs to be organized, cleaned, checked for accuracy, and sometimes spiced up with analytics or AI to make it truly valuable. In the end, it's delivered for people to use, maybe as dashboards, reports, APIs, or direct data feeds.

To make all that happen, you need a data product team, like the kitchen crew in a restaurant. It's a group of professionals with different skills who work together to bring the product to life. If any one of them is missing, things start to fall apart. These are the people who imagine the dish, do the cooking, keep the kitchen running smoothly, and constantly improve the menu. In most organizations, assembling such a team isn't simple. True enterprise data product teams often include people from different departments such as finance, analytics, engineering, and governance. Each is bringing their own expertise to create something that's not just technically sound, but genuinely useful and trusted.

Figure 15 below illustrates the typical composition of a data product team. It shows three levels of involvement: core, supporting, and periphery. These levels reflect how deeply each role is engaged in the day-to-day development and operation of the product.

Now, you might look at all these roles and feel a bit overwhelmed, as if every data product needs a full cast of ten people or more to make it work. That's not really the idea. Many of these roles can be combined or handled by the same person. For example, the solution architect and the data engineer might be the same person.

The key isn't having a separate person for every title, but ensuring the core responsibilities of each role are covered. What matters most is that someone on the team embodies or at least thinks like each role. If your data engineer is also acting as the solution architect, then they should think beyond just pipelines and transformations. They should also consider broader architectural questions, such as scalability, maintainability, and how their product fits within the company's ecosystem.

Data Product Team Composition

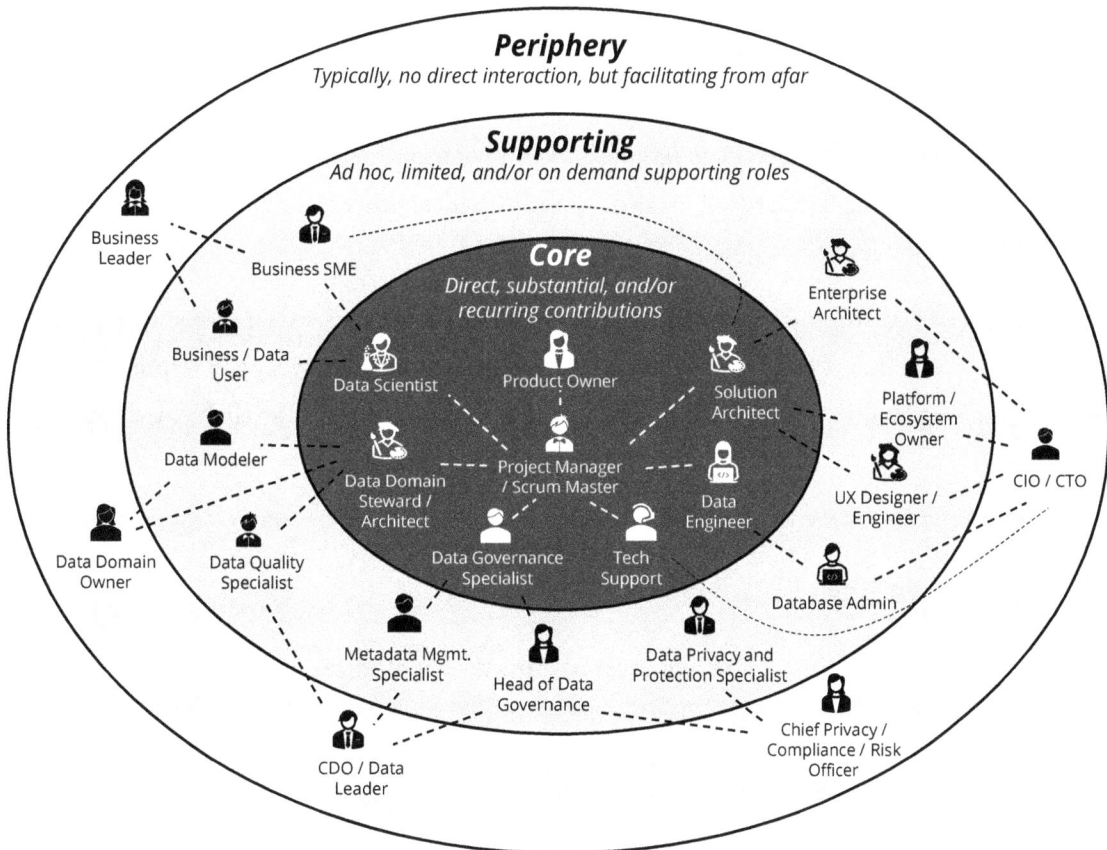

Figure 15 – An overview of commonly relevant roles in data product teams. Other roles that could be separately relevant but are not listed here include Quality Assurance (QA) Analyst/Tester, Data Visualization Expert, Network/Infrastructure Specialist, AI/ML Ops Engineer, and DevOps Engineer.

In some extreme cases, a data product might even be built and maintained by a single person. Whether that works depends on a few factors:

- **Organizational maturity:** In a small or early-stage organization, roles are often fluid, and one person wears many hats. In a mature enterprise, specialization tends to grow as processes and responsibilities become clearer. In younger or less formal setups, roles like Head of Data Governance or Data Domain Owner might not even exist yet, but that doesn't mean you can't get started. You can still apply the same principles by assigning those responsibilities informally to someone willing to take ownership and think with that mindset.

- **Product complexity:** A simple data product might not need a large team. A cross-domain product involving machine learning, real-time data, and strict compliance likely will.

- **Scale and criticality:** Products serving a handful of users can often be managed solo, but those supporting hundreds of users or business-critical processes require broader collaboration and oversight.

So, don't think of these roles as a staffing checklist. Think of them as essential perspectives that must be represented. Whether it's one person or ten, the goal is to make sure every key responsibility has someone thinking about it. That's what turns a simple data project into a reliable, well-governed data product.

3.1.1. Core Roles

At the center of Figure 15 are the core roles, representing the people directly responsible for building, maintaining, and continuously improving the data product. These individuals contribute hands-on and on a recurring basis, ensuring that design, delivery, and quality remain aligned with business needs:

- **Data Product Owner**: This role is central to the data product's success, encompassing ownership, advocacy, and strategic direction. The Data Product Owner crafts the vision, ensuring the product delivers value and meets user needs. They are responsible for assembling and leading the data product team, managing the product backlog, and acting as a liaison between stakeholders and developers. Reporting lines for this role vary, ranging from data teams to business units or data domain owners.

- **Project Manager/Scrum Master:** Serving the Data Product Owner, this role is crucial for orchestrating the project's workflow and timeline. In smaller setups, the Project Manager and Data Product Owner may be the same person. This role focuses on organizing activities, managing deadlines, and implementing Agile practices, with its importance tapering off post-data product launch.

- **Data Scientist**: Not always a necessary role, but important for products that embed AI, analytics, or data science. Data Scientists enrich the data product with insights derived from statistical analysis and machine learning, playing a key role in analyzing data, developing predictive models, and guiding decisions with their interpretations. If the data product heavily relies on AI or ML, there might be a separate role for an AI/ML Ops Engineer to focus on the operational aspect of deploying and maintaining machine learning models in production. For data products that rely heavily on reports and dashboards, there might be a dedicated Data Visualization Expert to present data clearly, intuitively, and visually appealingly.

- **Data Domain Steward/Architect**: This expert understands the nature of specific data types. Data domains like customer, product, or financial data are often organized into them. Among other things, they ensure data products don't overlap, that for each type of data there is a unique, trusted, or strategic source, and that any data ingested comes from the right source. They inject this kind of expertise into the design and management of the data product. The roles of steward and architect may be distinct or combined.

- **Data Governance Specialist**: This person serves as a liaison to the data governance team and ensures the data product aligns with organizational policies and standards. Depending on these policies and standards, responsibilities may include ensuring that the appropriate requirements for data quality, data modeling, metadata management, data cataloging, and privacy and security are incorporated into the design.

- **Tech Support**: A role that comes into play post-development, assisting users and consumers of the data product. Responsibilities include troubleshooting, system maintenance, and providing technical support, with a focus on resolving post-launch technical issues.

- **Data Engineer**: The foundational builder of the data product, creating the necessary infrastructure and pipelines for data processing and storage. This role involves developing, testing, and maintaining data management systems and applications. Data engineering is required to ingest data and make it available for consumption, tasks that might be handled by different engineers. Depending on the specific flavor of the data product, more specific data engineers might be part of the team, such as a DevOps engineer. For data products that rely on significant computational resources or cloud infrastructure, there may be a specific role for a Network/Infrastructure Specialist.

- **Solution Architect**: Responsible for the overarching design of the technical solution supporting the data product. This role includes designing scalable systems, integrating new technologies, and maintaining technical standards, ensuring that the technical aspects effectively support the data product's goals.

Together, these core roles act as the heartbeat of the data product. They blend technical know-how with product thinking, balancing user needs, governance requirements, and operational realities. More than anything, they are the ones most tactically helping each other day to day. They work together relatively closely, often in daily or regular check-ins, to move the product forward. Unlike supporting or periphery roles, they remain actively and consistently involved across nearly every phase of the data product's lifecycle.

3.1.2. Supporting Roles

Surrounding the core are the supporting roles. These are experts who engage on an intermittent or on-demand basis. Their input shapes the product's design, usability, and compliance, but they may not work on it daily. This doesn't mean they aren't deeply involved. Many of them contribute intensively at specific stages of the product's lifecycle. Compared to core roles, they typically step in during certain phases or when specific needs or issues arise, rather than remaining continuously involved from start to finish:

- **Business SME (Subject Matter Expert):** A specialist with deep knowledge of a particular business area. This person provides essential context for data use, ensuring that the data product delivers insights that actually matter. They help define business logic, validate outputs, and confirm that the product's metrics and dimensions reflect real-world business meaning.

- **Business/Data User:** The practical end-user who applies the data product in their daily work. They provide feedback on usability, accuracy, and value, helping ensure the product evolves in ways that serve real business needs. Their engagement is key to adoption and continuous improvement.

- **Data Modeler:** Designs the data structures that power the product. They ensure models are optimized for performance, aligned with enterprise data models, and flexible enough for future extensions. The data modeler works closely with engineers to translate conceptual and logical models into physical ones.

- **Data Quality Specialist:** The inspector who ensures the data is accurate and usable. Responsibilities include defining data quality criteria, performing data quality checks, and resolving data quality issues. Sometimes, there can be a related, separate role for a Quality Assurance (QA) Analyst/Tester to ensure that the data product is reliable, functional, and meets quality standards before it is released.

- **Metadata Management Specialist:** A role that is essential for ensuring that the right, minimally required metadata is captured, maintained, and democratized. This supports documenting data lineage and cataloging the data product.

- **Head of Data Governance:** Provides overarching guidance to ensure data products operate within an enterprise governance framework. Though not directly part of the team, this leader ensures that consistent policies, standards, and stewardship practices are in place for all data products.

- **Data Privacy and Protection Specialist:** Typically part of a dedicated privacy, legal, or security function. This role reviews the product's design, metadata, and workflows to confirm compliance with privacy, security, and ethical-use standards. They play a key role in risk assessments and are often consulted during escalations.

- **Database Administrator:** People in this role administer the upstream and downstream databases for the data product. Engagement with them is usually required to set up connections, facilitate authentication, and ensure interoperability.

- **UX Designer/Engineer:** The engineer who designs the user interface and experience for the data product, ensuring user-friendliness. This role is only needed when the data product has a specific UI/UX component. I've been involved with about 50 data products in the last year alone, and only once was this a separately dedicated role.

- **Platform/Ecosystem Owner:** Oversees the broader data or technology platform on which the data product operates. They ensure that the platform meets performance, scalability, and integration needs while maintaining alignment between product requirements and ecosystem capabilities.

- **Enterprise Architect:** The strategic thinker who ensures the data product fits within the organization's overall architecture and technology strategy. They review key design decisions to ensure scalability, security, and reuse, and help position major data products as reliable enterprise assets for multiple downstream consumers.

Supporting roles give the product team depth, adding expertise in areas like modeling, compliance, and user experience, especially at moments in the broader lifecycle when these matters most.

3.1.3. Periphery Roles

On the outer edge sit the periphery roles, who are the leaders and stakeholders who may not interact directly with the team but create the conditions that allow it to succeed. They provide strategic direction, funding, and organizational support:

- **Business Leader:** Provides overarching direction and resources for the data product. This role sets the strategic course, secures necessary funding, and champions the product across the organization. The business leader bridges strategy and execution, aligning the data product's goals with business priorities and ensuring its outcomes are recognized and valued.

- **Data Domain Owner:** Oversees governance and quality within a specific data domain, such as customer, product, or employee data. This role ensures consistency and strategic alignment across related data products and maintains awareness of both upstream and downstream dependencies. The domain owner helps prevent fragmentation and drives a unified approach to managing shared data products.

- **Chief Data Officer/Data Leader:** Plays a pivotal role, especially in organizations still maturing their data capabilities. While not directly involved in designing individual data products, the CDO sets the vision for how data products fit into the broader enterprise strategy. They build data culture, promote literacy, and evangelize the value of data products to business leaders, often serving as the key influencer who turns awareness into investment and long-term commitment.

- **Chief Privacy/Compliance/Risk Officer:** Sets the enterprise-wide vision, policies, and standards for privacy, compliance, and risk management. Though not part of day-to-day product operations, this leader ensures the right safeguards and accountability structures are in place. Their team, comprising privacy, legal, or security specialists, works closely with data product teams to ensure regulatory compliance and ethical use of data. They often step in during escalations or when high-risk issues surface.

- **CIO/CTO:** Defines the broader technology strategy and ensures architectural alignment across the organization. The CIO or CTO provides the platforms, tools, and patterns that enable consistent, scalable data product development. Their influence shapes the technical framework within which data products are designed, integrated, and operated, ensuring that innovation happens on solid, secure foundations.

These roles may not work directly with the product day to day, but their influence is vital. They ensure that the environment enables data products to thrive, and they become especially important when things are not working as planned. They handle escalations, enforce compliance, and secure emergency funding when needed. They can stand before the CEO or other senior leaders to make the case for continued investment and to highlight the strategic importance of data products. Perhaps most importantly, they provide sponsorship and drive the broader change management effort, especially in the early stages when success is not yet visible and clear to everyone.

3.2. Building a Portfolio of Data Products

Now that the right data product teams and roles are in place, the next challenge is scaling the effort beyond individual projects. A single successful data product is valuable, but Chief Data Officers (CDOs) and other data leaders must deliver value across many data products. How do you coordinate dozens of initiatives and ensure they're aligned to strategic goals? The answer is to take a portfolio approach. In this section, we outline how to build and manage a portfolio of data products so that your data strategy drives sustained business impact.

Many organizations are eager to develop data products, but identifying, building, and governing one data product is very different from doing so at an enterprise scale. Data leaders, especially CDOs, often grapple with how to mobilize an entire organization around data. They ask: Where do we start when managing data products at scale?

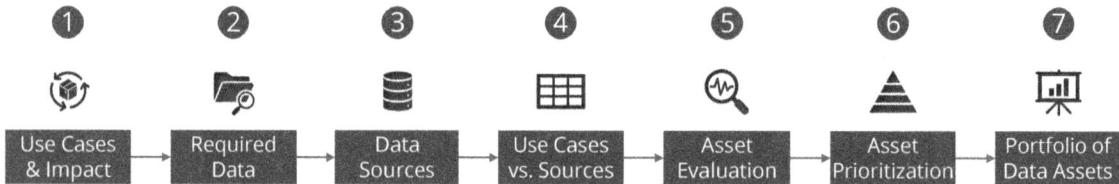

Figure 16 – The seven-step approach to data product portfolio management.

This section presents a step-by-step approach for taking a portfolio view of data products. Figure 16 presents a seven-step methodology for building and managing a data product portfolio. We will walk through each of the seven steps, explaining the approach and providing examples. By the end, you should see how a portfolio approach ensures that data efforts stay aligned with business needs and deliver measurable value.

3.2.1. Step 1: Use Cases and Impact

The first step is to identify the data-driven use cases that matter for your organization. You don't have to do this for the entire enterprise all at once. You can start with one domain or business line, and this might even be recommended.

Use cases are the specific mechanisms through which the overall organizational strategy can be implemented (Koenders, My Simple Data Strategy Framework, 2022). Data strategy and data governance do not add value in and of themselves; they only do so to the extent that broader strategic goals are achieved. Hence, use cases must be the first step.

There are various ways to go about this. You can internally build an inventory of use cases by interviewing business and analytics leaders. For your sector, you can cobble together an overview of use cases from external sources. Most success is usually had with a hybrid approach: bring in an external list of use cases, then refine it with internal leaders. For the purposes of this section, I've used ChatGPT to build the inventory, which is presented in Figure 17 below. For example, under Finance and Accounting, the fraud detection and prevention use case leverages real-time analytics and machine learning models on a combination of customer and transaction data to identify patterns and detect suspicious events. Or, under Marketing and Sales, as part of marketing mix modeling, the historical relationship between marketing efforts and sales performance is investigated to optimize the allocation of marketing budgets and the use of channels and tactics.

Data-driven Use Cases Across 15 Functional Areas

Finance & Accounting	Supply Chain Management	Business Development & Strategy
Financial forecasting and modeling	Supplier performance evaluation	Market entry and growth analysis
Real-time financial reporting	Route optimization for deliveries	Competitive intelligence
Fraud detection and prevention	Inventory turnover analysis	Partnership and acquisition target analysis
Capital expenditure optimization	Risk assessment for supply chain disruptions	Customer and market segmentation for new opportunities
Cash flow analysis	Optimal pricing strategies for logistics services	ROI evaluation for strategic investments
Expense tracking and analysis	**Research & Development**	**Health & Safety**
Operations & Production	Product success prediction	Incident and accident prediction and prevention
Production line optimization	Analysis of customer feedback for product improvement	Environmental impact tracking and optimization
Predictive maintenance for equipment	Competitor benchmarking and analysis	Safety compliance monitoring and reporting
Resource allocation and scheduling	Patent and IP landscape analysis	Worker health monitoring and intervention planning
Inventory optimization	Clinical trial data analysis	Disaster response and recovery planning
Process automation and streamlining	**Legal & Compliance**	**E-commerce & Web**
Cost reduction and efficiency analysis	Contract analysis and optimization	Shopping cart abandonment analysis
Human Resources	Regulatory compliance monitoring	Recommendation engine optimization
Talent analytics	Legal case outcome prediction	Web traffic source analysis and conversion optimization
Employee turnover prediction	IP infringement monitoring	A/B testing of website design elements
Compensation and benefits benchmarking	Data governance and data privacy compliance tracking	Price elasticity and promotional impact analysis
Employee engagement and sentiment analysis	**Customer Service & Support**	**Real Estate & Facility Management**
Training and development needs analysis	Customer satisfaction and NPS analysis	Space utilization and optimization
Diversity and inclusion metrics tracking	Call center optimization and voice analytics	Energy consumption analytics and optimization
Marketing & Sales	Resolution time analytics and optimization	Predictive maintenance for building infrastructure
Customer segmentation and targeting	Feedback collection and analysis	Tenant satisfaction and retention analysis
Campaign performance measurement and optimization	Predictive support	Market price analysis for property acquisition or sale
Marketing mix modeling	**Product Management**	**Sustainability & CSR**
Digital marketing attribution	Product usage analytics	Carbon footprint measurement and optimization
Sentiment analysis on brand mentions	Feature adoption rates	Supply chain sustainability monitoring
Customer journey mapping and analytics	A/B testing results analysis	Social impact measurement
Sales	Product-market fit assessment	Stakeholder sentiment analysis on CSR initiatives
Lead scoring and prioritization	Customer feedback aggregation	Resource consumption and waste analysis
Customer churn prediction		
Cross-selling and up-selling opportunity		
Sales territory design and optimization		
Sales performance analysis and benchmarking		
Sales forecasting		

Figure 17 – Overview of 90 data-driven use cases across 15 business and functional areas. Data generated by ChatGPT.

Having use cases is not enough; we need a sense of their importance. As outlined in Section 2.2. Value Quantification and Business Case, there are four critical ways use cases can drive value:

- Increase revenues.
- Reduce costs.
- Enhance customer experience.
- Mitigate risk.

Some list "drive innovation" as a fifth value driver, but in my view, that's just a matter of timelines, because any innovation is meant to eventually drive value through the four mechanisms mentioned above. Table 13 shows an overview of marketing-related use cases and the typical "top-line impact" associated with them. In fact, for the use case of *marketing mix modeling* that we had just introduced above, we see "1 to 2% top line impact." If your company averages $1 billion in revenues, these estimates suggest that *marketing mix modeling* can drive $10–20 million on top of that.

Use Case	Top line impact
Personalization	0.25 to 0.50%
Targeting	<0.25%
Customer lifetime value	0.25 to 0.50%
Cross-selling and upselling	1 to 3%
A/B testing	0.25 to 0.50%
Precision marketing	1 to 2%
Marketing mix modeling	1 to 2%
Predictive analytics	0.5 to 1%
Social media monitoring	<0.25%

Table 13 – A set of marketing use cases with the impact they typically have on overall enterprise revenues. Source: (Salem & Koenders, 2023).

At the end of Step 1, you have a set of use cases alongside their estimated impact on the organization.

3.2.2. Step 2: Required Data

In this step, we investigate what data is needed to power the identified use cases. The first step is to define the critical data inputs for each use case. For example, in *product line optimization* under Operations and Production, required data includes production volume, machine performance logs, and raw material availability. Or for *employee turnover prediction* under Human Resources, data is required from employee satisfaction surveys, exit interview feedback, and industry turnover rates.

Once you have a partial or complete list of use cases, respective SMEs or process owners can help clarify what data is needed. As your list of critical data inputs grows, you will reach a point at which you can start grouping the data by data type or domain. Within sectors and, to a lesser extent, across sectors, these data types and domains are quite stable. Data domains that are almost always applicable include Customer (or the equivalent, such as Student, Patient, or Member), Employee, and Finance, as most organizations serve some group of people, employ people to do so, and need to manage their budgets. Some other domains, like Supply Chain or Research and Safety Data, are more specific and may only apply if the organization manages a physical supply chain of products and materials.

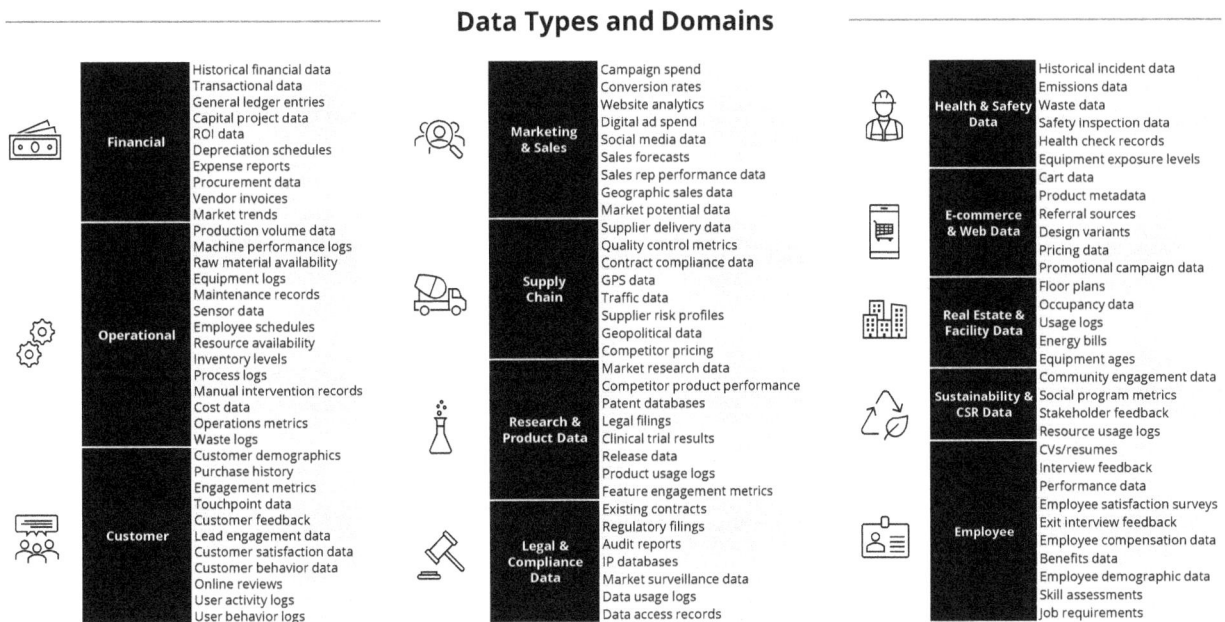

Data Types and Domains

Financial
- Historical financial data
- Transactional data
- General ledger entries
- Capital project data
- ROI data
- Depreciation schedules
- Expense reports
- Procurement data
- Vendor invoices
- Market trends

Operational
- Production volume data
- Machine performance logs
- Raw material availability
- Equipment logs
- Maintenance records
- Sensor data
- Employee schedules
- Resource availability
- Inventory levels
- Process logs
- Manual intervention records
- Cost data
- Operations metrics
- Waste logs

Customer
- Customer demographics
- Purchase history
- Engagement metrics
- Touchpoint data
- Customer feedback
- Lead engagement data
- Customer satisfaction data
- Customer behavior data
- Online reviews
- User activity logs
- User behavior logs

Marketing & Sales
- Campaign spend
- Conversion rates
- Website analytics
- Digital ad spend
- Social media data
- Sales forecasts
- Sales rep performance data
- Geographic sales data
- Market potential data

Supply Chain
- Supplier delivery data
- Quality control metrics
- Contract compliance data
- GPS data
- Traffic data
- Supplier risk profiles
- Geopolitical data
- Competitor pricing

Research & Product Data
- Market research data
- Competitor product performance
- Patent databases
- Legal filings
- Clinical trial results
- Release data
- Product usage logs
- Feature engagement metrics

Legal & Compliance Data
- Existing contracts
- Regulatory filings
- Audit reports
- IP databases
- Market surveillance data
- Data usage logs
- Data access records

Health & Safety Data
- Historical incident data
- Emissions data
- Waste data
- Safety inspection data
- Health check records
- Equipment exposure levels

E-commerce & Web Data
- Cart data
- Product metadata
- Referral sources
- Design variants
- Pricing data
- Promotional campaign data

Real Estate & Facility Data
- Floor plans
- Occupancy data
- Usage logs
- Energy bills
- Equipment ages

Sustainability & CSR Data
- Community engagement data
- Social program metrics
- Stakeholder feedback
- Resource usage logs

Employee
- CVs/resumes
- Interview feedback
- Performance data
- Employee satisfaction surveys
- Exit interview feedback
- Employee compensation data
- Benefits data
- Employee demographic data
- Skill assessments
- Job requirements

Figure 18 – Overview of data types and domains. Data generated by ChatGPT.

Figure 18 above shows what the result could be. There, 12 data domains are presented with about 100 sub-domains. All the organization's data can be mapped back to the types that are listed here. For example, Campaign Spend data under Marketing and Sales may include data on the initiatives and costs of digital advertising, traditional media campaigns, and sponsorships, and Sensor Data under Operational may include data from temperature sensors that are placed in storage areas and vibration sensors to monitor machinery health in factories.

Once you identify the critical data inputs for use cases and map them to data types or domains, you can build a matrix as shown in Figure 19. Above, we had the example use case of *product line optimization*, which maps to the Operational data domain, as it indeed requires operational data. In Figure 19, use cases are mapped to the broader data domains, which allows for visualization here, but in real life, you could (and should) map the use cases to the underlying, more granular sub-domains.

Functional or Business Area	Data-driven Use Case	Financial	Customer	Operational	Employee	Marketing & Sales	E-commerce & Web	Compliance & Legal	Sustainability & CSR	Supply Chain	Research & Product
Finance & Accounting	Financial forecasting and modeling	X									
	Real-time financial reporting	X									
	Fraud detection and prevention	X	X								
	Capital expenditure optimization	X									
	Cash flow analysis	X									
	Expense tracking and analysis	X									
Operations & Production	Production line optimization			X						X	
	Predictive maintenance for equipment			X							
	Resource allocation and scheduling	X		X	X						
	Inventory optimization			X							
	Process automation and streamlining			X							
	Cost reduction and efficiency analysis	X								X	
Human Resources	Talent analytics				X						
	Employee turnover prediction				X						
	Compensation and benefits benchmarking				X						
	Employee engagement and sentiment analysis				X						
	Training and development needs analysis				X						
	Diversity and inclusion metrics tracking				X						
Marketing	Customer segmentation and targeting		X			X	X				
	Campaign performance measurement and optimizati		X			X	X				
	Marketing mix modeling		X			X					
	Digital marketing attribution		X			X	X				
	Sentiment analysis on brand mentions		X								
	Customer journey mapping and analytics		X			X					
Sales	Sales forecasting		X			X					
	Lead scoring and prioritization		X			X					
	Customer churn prediction		X								
	Cross-selling and up-selling opportunity		X			X					
	Sales territory design and optimization					X					
	Sales performance analysis and benchmarking					X					
	Demand forecasting					X					
Supply Chain Management	Supplier performance evaluation							X		X	
	Route optimization for deliveries									X	
	Inventory turnover analysis	X		X						X	
	Risk assessment for supply chain disruptions							X		X	
	Optimal pricing strategies for logistics services	X				X				X	
Research & Development	Product success prediction										X
	Analysis of customer feedback for product improver		X								X
	Competitor benchmarking and analysis										X
	Patent and IP landscape analysis							X			
	Clinical trial data analysis							X			
Legal & Compliance	Contract analysis and optimization							X			
	Regulatory compliance monitoring							X			
	Legal case outcome prediction							X			
	IP infringement monitoring							X			
	Data governance and data privacy compliance tracki		X		X			X			
Customer Service & Support	Customer satisfaction and NPS analysis		X				X				
	Call center optimization and voice analytics		X								
	Resolution time analytics and optimization		X								
	Feedback collection and analysis		X								
	Predictive support		X								
Product Management	Product usage analytics										X
	Feature adoption rates	X			X						X
	A/B testing results analysis				X						X
	Product-market fit assessment		X								X
	Customer feedback aggregation		X		X						X

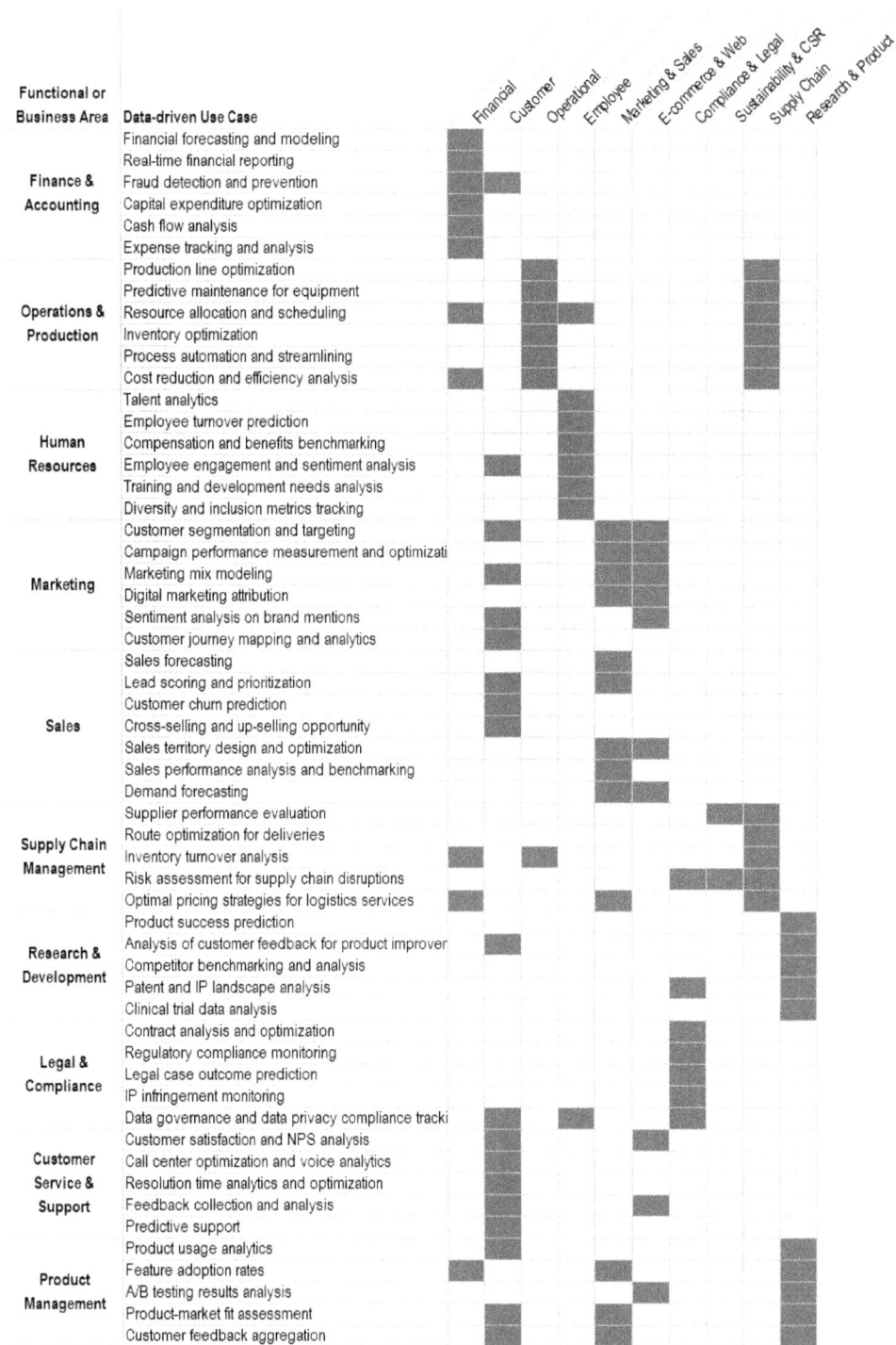

Figure 19 – Mapping of data-driven use cases against data types. Data generated by ChatGPT and refined by the author.

A panoramic understanding of just this, the key use cases mapped against the data types they require as inputs, is already invaluable for developing a data strategy and prioritizing specific data domains… but we're going to take this a lot further and make it even more actionable.

3.2.3. Step 3: Data Sources

Before we take the next step to identify source systems based on the (logical) data requirements from Step 2, let's assess the data requirements for one group of use cases. Table 14 below provides an overview of Marketing and Sales use cases and the critical data they rely on. This aligns with Figure 19, but at a higher level of granularity.

Use Cases		Critical Data Inputs
Marketing	**Customer segmentation and targeting**	Customer demographics, purchase history, engagement metrics
	Campaign performance measurement and optimization	Campaign spend, conversion rates, customer feedback
	Marketing mix modeling	Sales data, campaign data, external factors (e.g., economic indicators)
	Digital marketing attribution	Website analytics, digital ad spend, conversion tracking
	Sentiment analysis on brand mentions	Social media data, online reviews, press mentions
	Customer journey mapping and analytics	Touchpoint data, purchase data, customer feedback
Sales	**Sales forecasting**	Historical sales data, market trends, product launch data
	Lead scoring and prioritization	Lead engagement data, demographic data, prior purchase data
	Customer churn prediction	Customer satisfaction data, usage metrics, support ticket data
	Cross-selling and up-selling opportunity identification	Purchase history, customer preferences, product inventory
	Sales territory design and optimization	Sales rep performance data, geographic sales data, market potential data
	Sales performance analysis and benchmarking	Individual sales metrics, team metrics, industry benchmarks

Table 14 – Use cases for Marketing and Sales, and the critical data they require as inputs. Data generated by ChatGPT.

For example, we see that for the first use case of *customer segmentation and targeting*, data on customer demographics is needed. For the company in question, that data is stored in a physical system called *Global CRM*. Similarly, the Purchase History data that the same use case needs is stored in two systems: *E-commerce Transaction History* and *Retail Point of Sale System.* And so on and so forth. If we take all the critical data inputs from Table 14 above, and identify the source systems, we get the table shown in Table 15. As you can see, some data sources contain multiple types of critical data. For example, the *Global CRM Master* contains Customer Demographics, but also Customer Preferences, Customer Feedback, and Customer Segmentation Data.

Critical Data Input	Data Source(s)
Customer demographics	Global CRM Master, Market Research Database
Purchasing history	E-commerce Transaction History, Retail Point of Sale System
Lead engagement data	Marketing Automation Platform, Website Analytics Tool
Customer feedback	Customer Feedback Portal, Global CRM Master
Marketing campaign data	Marketing Performance Dashboard, Social Media Analytics
Web analytics data	Google Analytics, Adobe Analytics
Digital ad performance data	Google Ads Data, Facebook Ads Manager
Brand mentions	Social Media Monitoring Tool, News Aggregator Platform
E-commerce transaction data	E-commerce Backend System, Shopify Analytics
Sales data	Salesforce US Sales Data, SAP Europe Sales Data
Customer support interaction data	Customer Support Portal, Helpdesk Software
Market research data	Market Research Database, Nielsen Insights
Social media engagement data	Hootsuite Analytics, Instagram Insights
Email engagement data	Mailchimp Email Marketing Platform
Event attendance data	Event Management System, Webinar Software Data
Product usage data	Product Analytics Platform, Mobile App Analytics
Competitive intelligence data	Competitive Analysis Tool, SEMrush Data
Customer preferences	Global CRM Master, Customer Feedback Portal
Customer segmentation data	Market Segmentation Analysis Tool, Global CRM Master
Territory sales performance data	Salesforce US Dashboard, SAP Europe Sales Overview
Product interest data	Product Wishlist Database, E-commerce Backend System

Table 15 – Critical data inputs for Marketing and Sales use cases mapped against the source systems of that data. Data generated by ChatGPT.

3.2.4. Step 4: Use Cases versus Sources

We identified the required data for use cases (Step 2) and then mapped that against source systems (Step 3). The next view that can now be created is the mapping of use cases to source systems, as shown in Figure 22 below for Marketing and Sales.

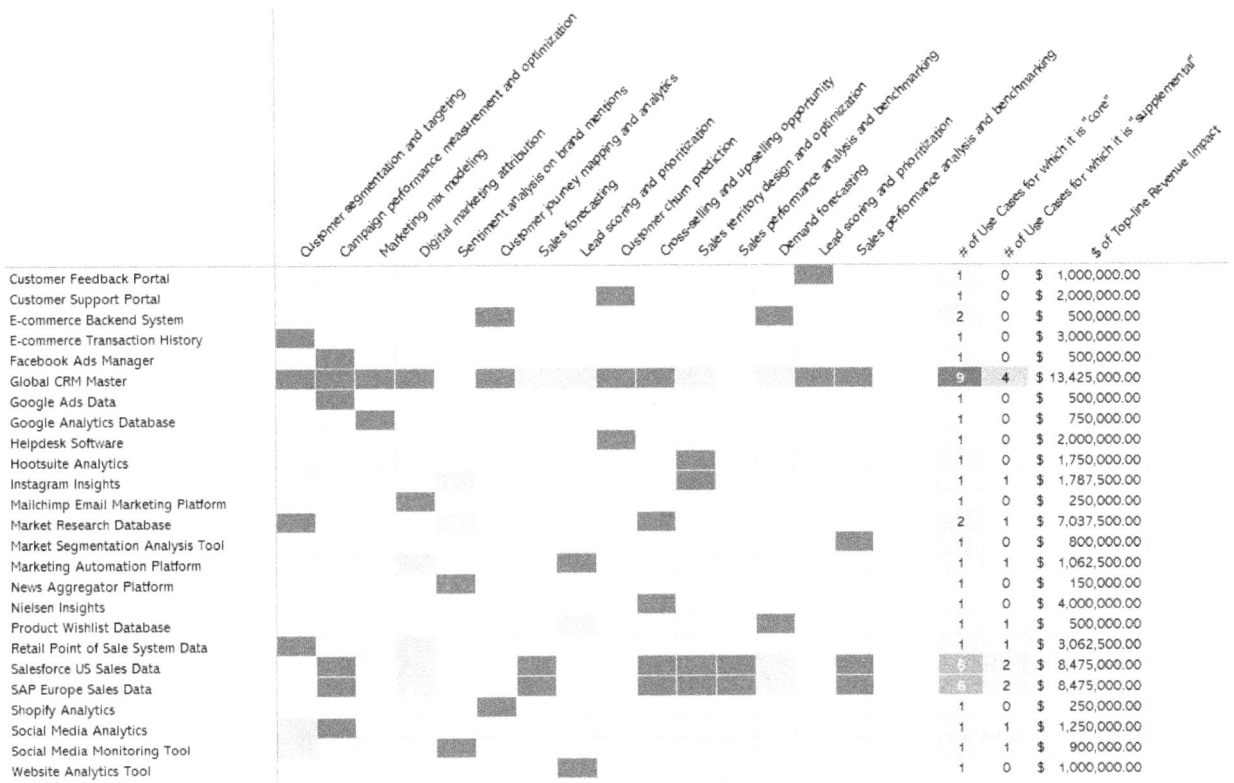

Source System	# of Use Cases for which it is "core"	# of Use Cases for which it is "supplemental"	$ of Top-line Revenue Impact
Customer Feedback Portal	1	0	$ 1,000,000.00
Customer Support Portal	1	0	$ 2,000,000.00
E-commerce Backend System	2	0	$ 500,000.00
E-commerce Transaction History	1	0	$ 3,000,000.00
Facebook Ads Manager	1	0	$ 500,000.00
Global CRM Master	9	4	$ 13,425,000.00
Google Ads Data	1	0	$ 500,000.00
Google Analytics Database	1	0	$ 750,000.00
Helpdesk Software	1	0	$ 2,000,000.00
Hootsuite Analytics	1	0	$ 1,750,000.00
Instagram Insights	1	1	$ 1,787,500.00
Mailchimp Email Marketing Platform	1	0	$ 250,000.00
Market Research Database	2	1	$ 7,037,500.00
Market Segmentation Analysis Tool	1	0	$ 800,000.00
Marketing Automation Platform	1	1	$ 1,062,500.00
News Aggregator Platform	1	0	$ 150,000.00
Nielsen Insights	1	0	$ 4,000,000.00
Product Wishlist Database	1	1	$ 500,000.00
Retail Point of Sale System Data	1	1	$ 3,062,500.00
Salesforce US Sales Data	6	2	$ 8,475,000.00
SAP Europe Sales Data	6	2	$ 8,475,000.00
Shopify Analytics	1	0	$ 250,000.00
Social Media Analytics	1	1	$ 1,250,000.00
Social Media Monitoring Tool	1	1	$ 900,000.00
Website Analytics Tool	1	0	$ 1,000,000.00

Figure 20 – Mapping use cases against source systems. Data generated by ChatGPT.

Here, the relative darkness of the cell reflects importance: the darker the cell, the more critical the data is for the use case; lighter cells indicate supporting or optional data. For example, for *customer segmentation and targeting*, data from the *Global CRM Master* is critical, but data from *Social Media Analytics* is 'nice-to-have'.

But we already know a lot more about the use cases. In fact, in Step 1 above, the very first thing we did was identify the use cases and the incremental revenue they could drive. This now enables us to say something about the value creation that is dependent on specific data sources. Because if we know that a given dataset is critical to three use cases estimated to drive two, three, and five million dollars in incremental revenue, we can say that ten million dollars in revenue depends on this dataset.

You cannot complete this exercise in isolation; you'll need to engage the respective use case and business process SMEs and owners. It might take some time to identify these people, but once you've found them, you will typically find them to be cooperative because they have a stake in ensuring that the use case is successful, and therefore, to clarify what data is critical and the impact that it can drive.

As you go along, you can start building an overview, as shown on the right-hand side of Figure 20, where the top-line revenue impact is estimated across all data sources critical to Marketing and Sales use cases. Beware of double-counting and make sure you explain and qualify the numbers appropriately. For example, if a given use case with a value-creation potential of $1 million depends on two data sources, you cannot say that the two data sources together drive $2 million.

3.2.5. Step 5: Data Product Evaluation

In the previous step, we mapped use cases and the value they drive against a set of data sources. Now we know that these data sources can drive value; they have inherent value for the company and can be considered data products.

While Figure 20 is already very insightful, it does not yet enable us to prioritize certain data products (and the investments in them) over others. If a given data product can deliver significant value but is already in place and "fit-for-purpose," no further action may be needed.

Figure 21 presents four data product assessment statuses, ranging from "fit-for-purpose" to "missing or large gaps," that enable a consistent evaluation of the data products. Here, fit-for-purpose should be interpreted broadly. On the positive end of the spectrum, it means that the right data is readily available at the right granularity and timeliness, is high-quality and reliable, and the source system is never down. On the other hand, it means that either the data product is not there at all, or, if it is, the data is highly deficient, unreliable, and/or incomplete.

++	Fit for purpose
+	Minor gaps or issues
-	Partially in place; moderate issues
--	Missing or large gaps

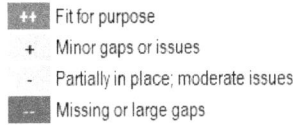

Figure 21 – Data product assessment values.

The next section (3.3. Maturity Models) provides a complete and more structured framework for measuring the maturity and performance of data products. You can use that maturity model to substitute or supplement the simpler status categories shown here. We now have the tools needed to build a so-called *heat map*, where data product assessment values are used to identify the greatest opportunities for value creation. These occur where assessment results show partial coverage or significant gaps, indicating that critical use cases cannot fully rely on the data they need. As a result, these areas directly constrain business impact and help prioritize where data product investments will have the most effect. See Figure 22 below.

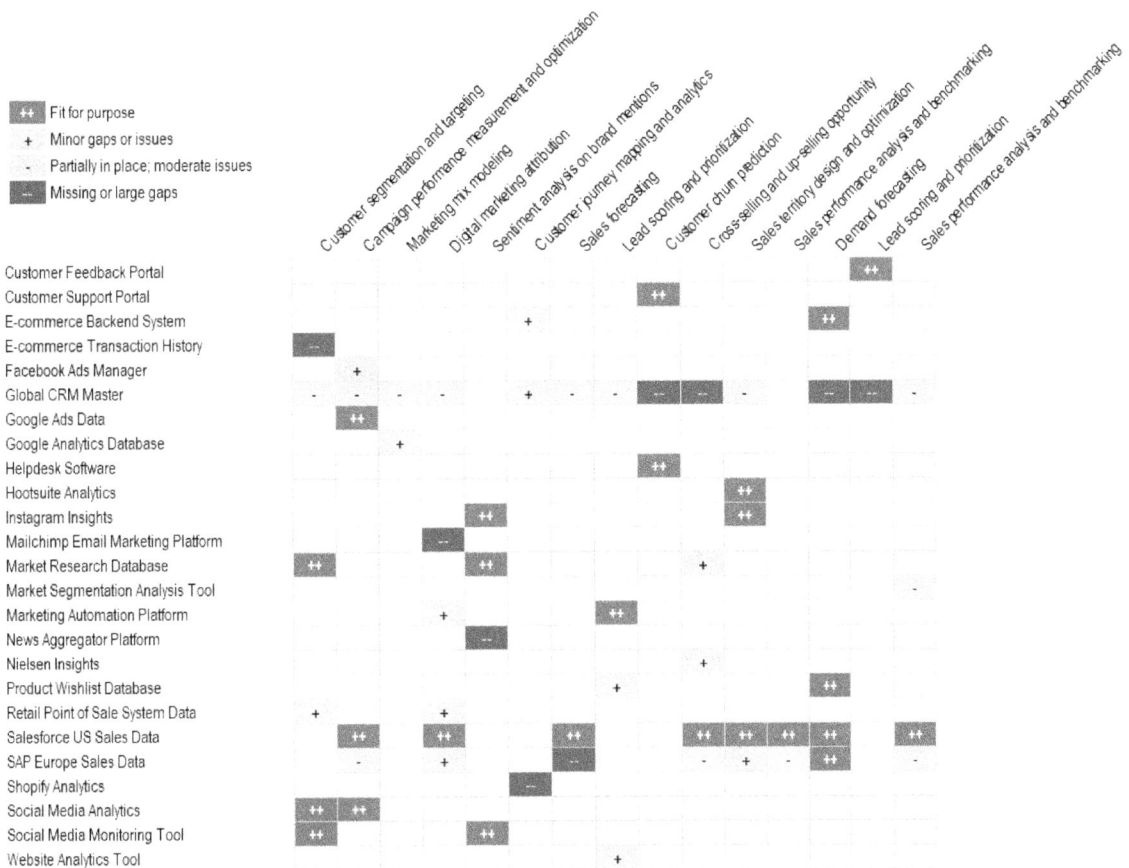

++	Fit for purpose
+	Minor gaps or issues
-	Partially in place; moderate issues
--	Missing or large gaps

	Customer segmentation and targeting	Campaign performance measurement and optimization	Marketing mix modeling	Digital marketing attribution	Sentiment analysis on brand mentions	Customer journey mapping and analytics	Sales forecasting	Lead scoring and prioritization	Customer churn prediction	Cross-selling and up-selling opportunity	Sales territory design and optimization	Sales performance analysis and benchmarking	Demand forecasting	Lead scoring and prioritization	Sales performance analysis and benchmarking
Customer Feedback Portal														++	
Customer Support Portal									++						
E-commerce Backend System						+							++		
E-commerce Transaction History	--														
Facebook Ads Manager		+													
Global CRM Master	-	-	-	-		+	-	-	--	--	-		--	--	-
Google Ads Data		++													
Google Analytics Database			+												
Helpdesk Software									++						
Hootsuite Analytics											++				
Instagram Insights					++						++				
Mailchimp Email Marketing Platform				--											
Market Research Database	++				++					+					
Market Segmentation Analysis Tool															-
Marketing Automation Platform				+				++							
News Aggregator Platform					--										
Nielsen Insights										+					
Product Wishlist Database								+					++		
Retail Point of Sale System Data	+			+											
Salesforce US Sales Data		++		++			++			++	++	++	++		++
SAP Europe Sales Data		-		+			--			-	+	-	++		-
Shopify Analytics						--									
Social Media Analytics	++	++													
Social Media Monitoring Tool	++				++										
Website Analytics Tool								+							

Figure 22 – A "heat map" of use cases against data products.

3.2.6. Step 6: Data Product Prioritization

The next step is to prioritize the data products based on everything we now know about them. Figure 23 presents the same heat map as in Figure 22, but we added back the revenue impact and the number of dependent use cases. We then reordered the data products in descending order by total revenue impact.

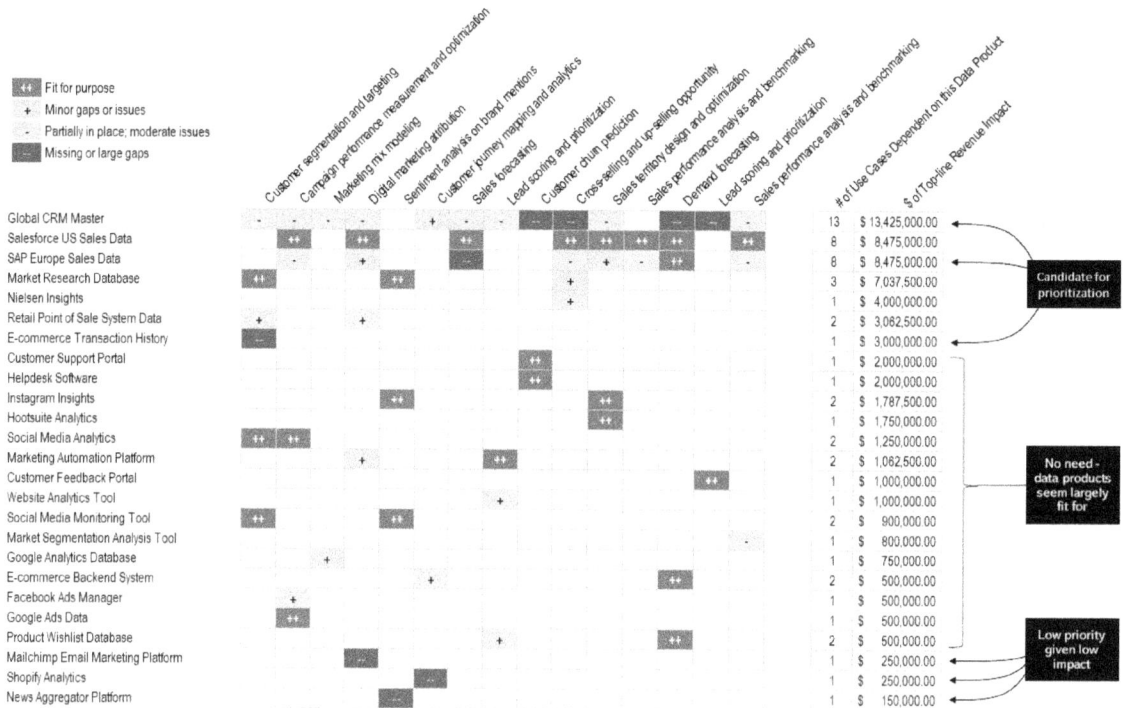

Figure 23 – Heat map of use cases against data products and the value they drive.

Now it's clearer which data products could be prioritized for enhancements and investments. For example, it is clear that the *Global CRM Master* is a big problem, as it is not optimally feeding nine (!) use cases, resulting in an impact of over $13 million. Various data products, such as *Instagram Insights*, the *Customer Support Portal*, and *Google Ads Data*, are fit-for-purpose and therefore don't seem to require remediation. And then we have a few at the bottom, like *Shopify Analytics* and *News Aggregator Platform*, that may not be in place but only support one use case each, with a limited impact.

If you were a Chief Data Officer and this panorama reflected the data products and use cases of your organization in a given domain, an impact-driven roadmap would open up for you. There is a clear opportunity to take one or two data products and use them as strategic locations to enhance the governance of strategically important data. This can be used to embed and operationalize various data governance capabilities, such as data ownership and stewardship, metadata management, and data quality, because each is critical to ensuring that data products are adequately governed.

3.2.7. Step 7: Portfolio of Data Products

It is a commonly cited fact that the expected tenure of data leaders like Chief Data Officers is short, on average, less than 2.5 years. To a large extent, this is explained by the fact that CDOs struggle to achieve meaningful business impact in the short- to medium-term.

That is exactly why the approach outlined here is so powerful. If you prioritize data products using the logic presented in Steps 1–6, you are almost guaranteed to generate an impact. And as you start with use cases and their impact, you engage the business and functional areas from the get-go, and therefore avoid falling into the trap of "doing data for the sake of data," which will go a long way to avoid the perception that data governance is a cost and hindrance to the business.

You're not done here. The data products that you have identified are analogous to the properties in a real estate portfolio (Koenders, 2023). You need to actively manage them, ensuring they are kept up to date, that data users remain satisfied, that new requirements are incorporated as they arise, and that value generation is not assumed but explicitly tracked over time.

Figure 24 below shows the organization's data product portfolio dashboard from this point of view. It shows the number of certified data products, the number of use cases mapped to them, and the value created through incremental revenue and risk mitigation.

In the center, you see a graph that tracks the number of certified data products over time and, more critically, the number of enabled use cases and their associated impact, expressed in revenue. This is key to CDO career longevity: being able to evidence the value created through targeted data enablement and governance activities.

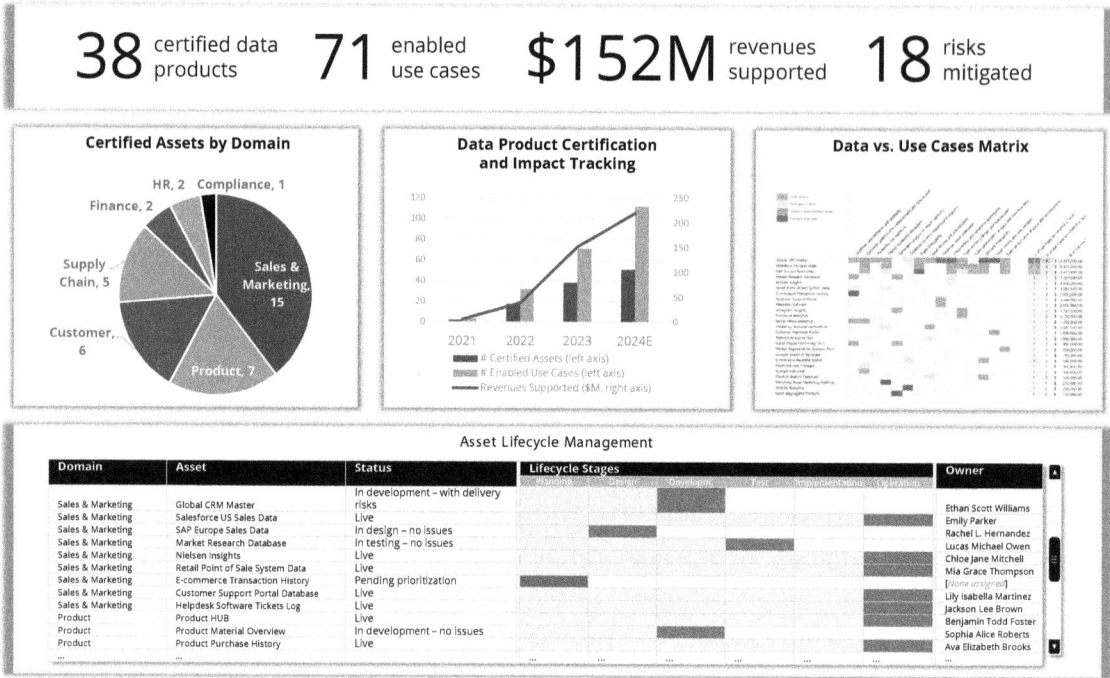

Figure 24 – A dashboard for data products.

At the bottom, you can see a pipeline view of the data products. Some of them are being pushed through a structured activation lifecycle, while others are live already. You'll see that the *Global CRM Master* that we investigated earlier has indeed been prioritized; it is currently in the "development" phase.

3.2.8. Anecdote from the Marketplace

I've used and refined this approach working with multiple companies across Europe and the US, and across banking, insurance, retail, technology, and manufacturing. In one example in the manufacturing sector, we followed a slightly altered version of the seven steps outlined here. Given that it was a complex, global company, identifying use cases across the entire organization was not feasible. Instead, we picked one business domain as our primary focus, namely the commercial division, and then the sub-domains of marketing and sales (not unlike the scope of use cases in step three above).

We identified a set of ~30 use cases, most of which had already been defined for other purposes. We executed a light, accelerated version of Steps 2–4 to identify the required data and corresponding sources, and to map use cases to the sources. We skipped ahead to step five and engaged the use case owners and SMEs, asking whether they had access to the right, fit-for-purpose data. If not, then what data or source was missing? What was the issue?

We quickly identified eight use cases consistently held back by data issues and found that two specific data sources were causing problems in six of them. We got to work. Together with the central data team and the commercial team, we aligned on owners for the two data sources, assessed them against a set of formal certification criteria, and drafted a plan to address the gaps.

Fast forward a few months, and the first data product had been enhanced and certified to meet the needs of the documented use cases. At the time of writing, the exact impact had yet to be measured (as it takes time for the impact to be realized), but initial anecdotal evidence suggested that marketing effectiveness may have increased by high single or even double-digit percentages. In any case, the CDO in question was able to introduce and refine the approach, deliver a modest win, and kickstart a broader roadmap with additional data products, use cases, and domains.

3.3. Maturity Models

Maturity models are among the most practical tools you can use to understand where you stand today and what it takes to improve.

> *In their simplest form, they describe what "good" looks like across different areas and give you a way to assess how far along you are.*

I've personally led well over 50 of these assessments in my career, and I've seen, again and again, how powerful they can be when done right. They give structure to conversations that would otherwise stay subjective or vague, and they help teams make decisions based on facts rather than opinions.

A good maturity model helps in two main ways. First, it provides a factual framework to guide improvement. When you want to strengthen how data products are designed, built, and adopted, it helps to know what "mature" actually means, and how you compare against it. Second, it helps you track progress over time. Once you assess where you are and define where you want to be, you can hold yourself and your organization accountable for making measurable progress.

In this section, we'll go through two maturity models that, together, give a complete picture. The first focuses on the maturity of individual data products and how well each one performs across key dimensions such as usability, quality, and automation. The second looks at the organization's overall maturity and how ready and capable it is to drive a data-product-driven way of working. Both models are explained in detail, along with examples and structures you can immediately apply within your own organization.

3.3.1. Maturity Framework for Individual Data Products

So far, we've discussed how to design and manage data products within a broader portfolio. But once you've reached that stage, once you truly start managing data products at a portfolio level, you also need a structured way to look at the performance of each individual product within that portfolio. It's just like managing a real estate portfolio: you wouldn't want to see only the total value of all properties combined; you'd want to know which houses are in great shape, which need maintenance, and which are sitting idle. The same logic applies to data products.

That's where assessing the maturity of individual data products comes in. If you can consistently and systematically evaluate how each product is performing, it becomes much easier to manage the entire portfolio with confidence. You'll know where to invest, where to improve, and where to retire or rethink.

But to truly understand whether an individual data product is successful, you need a way to measure its performance, especially from the perspective of its users and the value it creates. That's exactly what this section is about. We'll introduce a simple, structured framework to measure the maturity of individual data products, explain what each dimension means, and then apply it to a practical example.

Why do you need such a framework? Because the word *product* implies something that has consumers. A car, a pair of shoes, a phone—each has to be used and appreciated to be considered successful. The same logic applies to data products. You might have invested time and resources into building one, but if people aren't finding it, using it, or gaining value from it, then it's not fulfilling its purpose. And just as with physical products, what works today might not meet users' needs next year. Business needs change, technology evolves, and expectations rise.

That's why you need a structured way to check whether each data product continues to drive value, justify its investment, and evolve with its consumers. A maturity framework does exactly that. Think of it as a scorecard: a consistent, repeatable way to evaluate how well a data product is performing across key areas. It doesn't matter if it's a massive analytical dataset with millions of records or a small, static reference table that updates once a year. Every data product can be held against the same baseline to ensure it's adopted, trusted, and delivering measurable value.

This is not measurement for the sake of measurement. It's a practical tool for identifying where attention is needed to sustain and grow value. Because here's the key insight: if even one dimension of a data product lags, the product's ability to generate value is at risk. But the reverse is also true. If all dimensions are developed to at least a sufficient level, then value creation isn't just possible—it's guaranteed. Let's now look at the actual dimensions that make up this maturity framework. Many of these may feel familiar, as they intentionally build on and extend the key data product properties described in Section 1.2, translating them into measurable indicators of maturity:

1. **Awareness:** People need to know that a data product exists and understand what it's for. If users don't know about it, they can't use it or ask for it. Awareness is the first step toward any kind of adoption or value creation.

2. **Understandability:** Users should be able to easily grasp what the data product contains, what it represents, and how to interpret it. Clear documentation, examples, and definitions make the product approachable. If users can't understand it, they'll avoid using it altogether.

3. **Interoperability:** A strong data product doesn't stand alone; it connects easily with other data. It should be simple to join or integrate with related datasets, analytics tools, and

applications. This flexibility allows teams to reuse and build on it, multiplying its usefulness.

4. **Trust:** People must believe the data is reliable, accurate, and secure. If they doubt its quality or consistency, they won't use it for important decisions. Trust takes time to build, but it is the single biggest driver of sustained use.

5. **Actionability:** Once users have access to and trust the data, they should be able to act on it immediately. The data product should be clean, well-structured, and ready for direct use, and not something that requires heavy preparation, reformatting, or recalculation. A truly actionable product saves time and reduces friction between insight and action.

6. **Adoption:** The actual usage, such as how many people and processes rely on the data product day-to-day. You can see it in access logs, reports, and collaboration across teams. Widespread, consistent use is the clearest sign that a data product has earned its place in the organization.

7. **Business Impact:** The measurable value the product creates, whether that's revenue growth, cost reduction, time savings, or better decisions. High impact doesn't always require high adoption; sometimes a single use case can deliver massive value. What matters is that the impact can be shown and tied back to the data product.

8. **Product Orientation:** Every data product should be managed like a true product with ownership, iteration, and care for the user's experience. It's not a one-time project but something that evolves as needs change. A product mindset keeps it relevant, reliable, and continuously improving.

Now, if we want to move from understanding these dimensions to actually assessing maturity (scoring them), we need to introduce a maturity framework. In practice, this means defining what "good" and "bad" look like for each dimension: what characterizes low maturity and what signals that a data product has reached a high level of maturity. Many maturity models use four or five levels, but to keep things simple and practical for this book, we'll use two—the two ends of the spectrum. Table 16 below shows what low and high maturity look like for each of the dimensions we just defined.

Dimension	Low Maturity	High Maturity
Awareness	Few people know the data product exists. It's buried in systems or shared informally, with no visibility or communication.	The data product is well-known and visible across relevant teams. It's listed in catalogs or marketplaces, actively promoted, and referenced in documentation and meetings. Users know where to find it and what it's for.
Understandability	Users struggle to understand what the data means, where it comes from, or how to interpret it. There's little to no documentation or examples.	The purpose, content, and meaning of the data are clear. Business definitions, examples, and data dictionaries are available. Users can confidently interpret and explain it to others without external help.
Interoperability	The data product exists in isolation and can't easily be connected to other data or tools. Integrating it requires manual work or custom code.	The product is built with standardized formats, shared identifiers, and APIs. It connects smoothly to analytics tools and other data products. Teams can combine and reuse it easily for new use cases.
Trust	Data quality is uncertain, and users question accuracy or security. Different teams might get different results from the same data.	The product is reliable, consistent, and secure. Quality checks, lineage, and ownership are visible. Users trust it enough to make critical business decisions without hesitation.
Actionability	Users must clean, reshape, or recalculate data before using it. It's too raw or incomplete for direct application.	The data is ready to use as-is. It's clean, well-structured, and directly applicable to known use cases. Users can take it and immediately apply it without extra transformation work.
Adoption	Few people use it, and usage is inconsistent or ad hoc. There's little evidence of recurring or cross-team engagement.	The product is actively and broadly used across teams and processes. Access logs show regular activity, and it's referenced in dashboards, reports, or applications. It's part of daily operations.
Business Impact	The data product's value is unclear or anecdotal. There's no measurement of outcomes tied to it.	The product delivers clear, measurable impact, such as revenue growth, cost savings, efficiency gains, or risk reduction. Impact is tracked, reported, and linked back to specific use cases.
Product Orientation	The product is treated as a one-off project with no clear owner or roadmap. It decays over time and doesn't evolve with user needs.	The product has a defined owner, roadmap, and feedback loop. It's actively managed and improved over time based on user input and business priorities. It stays relevant, reliable, and well-supported.

Table 16 – Overview of data maturity interpretations across dimensions.

Now that we've defined the framework and clarified what low and high maturity look like across each dimension, we can make this more tangible by looking at two examples. We'll apply the framework to two very different data products to see how it works in practice.

Let's take a fictional company called Nordex Supply Group, a mid-sized manufacturer and distributor of home appliances operating across North America and Europe. Nordex manages complex supply chains with multiple production sites, regional warehouses, and retail partners. Over the past two years, they've started building a more structured portfolio of data products to help manage operations, improve fulfillment accuracy, and reduce working capital. Among their growing portfolio, two data products stand out for their projected business impact: the Inventory and Stock Movement Data Product, and the Sales Orders and Returns Data Product.

The Inventory and Stock Movement Data Product serves as the single source of truth for tracking item availability across Nordex's eight regional warehouses and three main production sites. It integrates daily extracts from the ERP system (SAP S/4HANA), warehouse management software, and shipping providers. The data is stored in Snowflake and refreshed every six hours. Each record reflects an item's stock status, including current quantity on hand, items in transit, and those reserved for pending sales orders. Historical data goes back 24 months, allowing users to track trends and identify recurring stock issues. Supply chain planners and finance analysts consume the data to optimize restocking cycles and reduce inventory carrying costs.

In Figure 25 below, you can see the maturity assessment of the Inventory and Stock Movement Data Product. The visual summarizes how this data product performs across the eight maturity dimensions. A few areas show solid performance, notably understandability, interoperability, and actionability, which confirm that the data itself is well-integrated and easy to use once accessed.

The main challenges, however, lie at the beginning and the end of the value chain. Awareness, adoption, and business impact all score low, indicating that even though the data product is technically strong, its value remains underutilized. In practice, adoption and impact are often trailing indicators, which are symptoms of deeper issues elsewhere. Here, the real issue seems to be awareness. The product is sound and actionable, but people simply don't know it exists or how to use it. There is also no clearly assigned owner. Given that an owner should advocate for it, promote its benefits, and build user engagement, a logical next step for this data product would be to assign a formal owner and empower that person to increase its visibility across teams. Doing so would almost certainly drive greater adoption and measurable business impact.

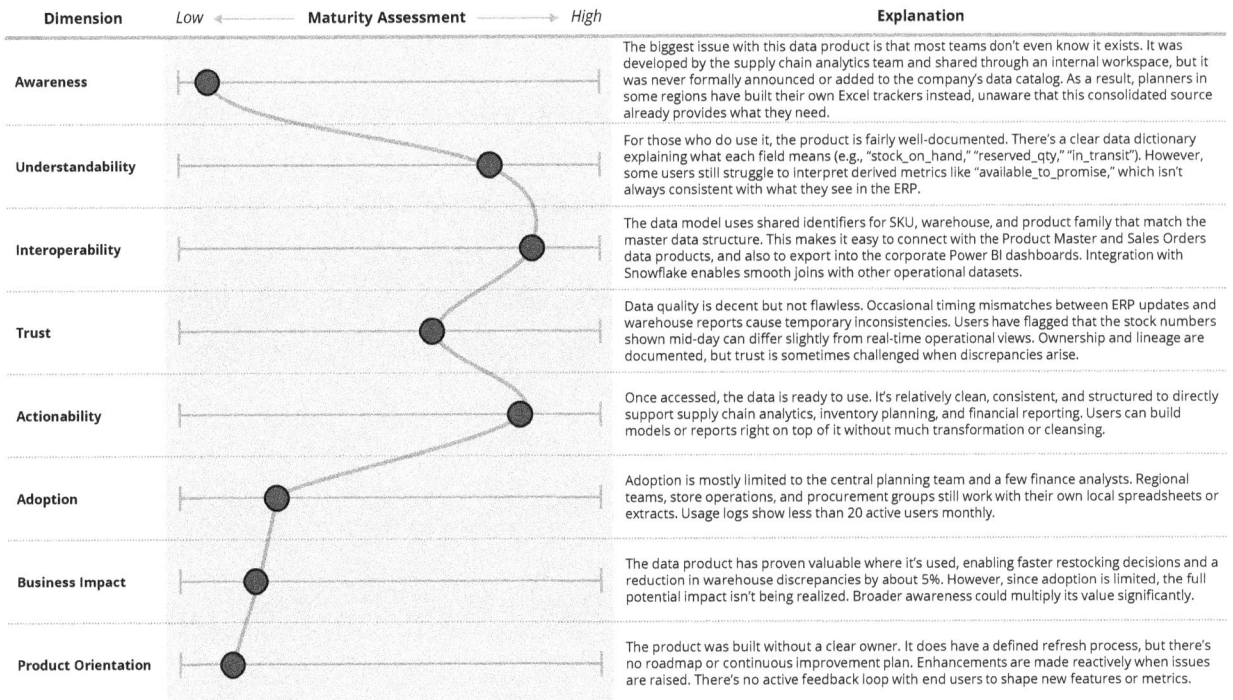

Dimension	Low ← Maturity Assessment → High	Explanation
Awareness		The biggest issue with this data product is that most teams don't even know it exists. It was developed by the supply chain analytics team and shared through an internal workspace, but it was never formally announced or added to the company's data catalog. As a result, planners in some regions have built their own Excel trackers instead, unaware that this consolidated source already provides what they need.
Understandability		For those who do use it, the product is fairly well-documented. There's a clear data dictionary explaining what each field means (e.g., "stock_on_hand," "reserved_qty," "in_transit"). However, some users still struggle to interpret derived metrics like "available_to_promise," which isn't always consistent with what they see in the ERP.
Interoperability		The data model uses shared identifiers for SKU, warehouse, and product family that match the master data structure. This makes it easy to connect with the Product Master and Sales Orders data products, and also to export into the corporate Power BI dashboards. Integration with Snowflake enables smooth joins with other operational datasets.
Trust		Data quality is decent but not flawless. Occasional timing mismatches between ERP updates and warehouse reports cause temporary inconsistencies. Users have flagged that the stock numbers shown mid-day can differ slightly from real-time operational views. Ownership and lineage are documented, but trust is sometimes challenged when discrepancies arise.
Actionability		Once accessed, the data is ready to use. It's relatively clean, consistent, and structured to directly support supply chain analytics, inventory planning, and financial reporting. Users can build models or reports right on top of it without much transformation or cleansing.
Adoption		Adoption is mostly limited to the central planning team and a few finance analysts. Regional teams, store operations, and procurement groups still work with their own local spreadsheets or extracts. Usage logs show less than 20 active users monthly.
Business Impact		The data product has proven valuable where it's used, enabling faster restocking decisions and a reduction in warehouse discrepancies by about 5%. However, since adoption is limited, the full potential impact isn't being realized. Broader awareness could multiply its value significantly.
Product Orientation		The product was built without a clear owner. It does have a defined refresh process, but there's no roadmap or continuous improvement plan. Enhancements are made reactively when issues are raised. There's no active feedback loop with end users to shape new features or metrics.

Figure 25 – Maturity assessment of the Inventory and Stock Movement data product.

Let's turn to a second sample data product. The Sales Orders and Returns Data Product combines data from the company's e-commerce platform, point-of-sale integrations, and customer service systems. It provides a unified view of all sales orders, fulfillment status, and return events, refreshed every night. Each row represents an individual transaction line item, including customer ID, SKU, quantity, order date, shipment date, and reason for return (if applicable). The data resides in the same Snowflake environment, with built-in lineage linking back to the customer and product master data products. Commercial teams use it to analyze sales performance by channel and to identify product quality or fulfillment issues driving returns.

In Figure 26 below, you can see the maturity assessment of the Sales Orders and Returns Data Product. The results tell a very different story from the previous example. Here, awareness, adoption, and interoperability all score high. Everyone knows about this data product, uses it regularly, and can easily connect it to other sources. On paper, this looks like a success story. However, the real issue sits at the heart of the product: data quality. Users have become wary of inconsistencies between this dataset and the underlying ERP system, which has eroded trust. Even though people continue to use the product, they do so cautiously, often double-checking numbers or reconciling reports manually.

As a result, the business impact remains far below its potential. The product is technically well-built and highly visible, but poor quality prevents it from being treated as a true source of truth. The next step for Nordex is clear: this data product doesn't need more users or better marketing; it needs stronger governance and active quality management. Assigning a dedicated data steward, implementing automated quality checks, and tightening synchronization with the ERP could directly restore confidence. Once trust is rebuilt, the existing awareness and adoption will naturally convert into tangible business impact.

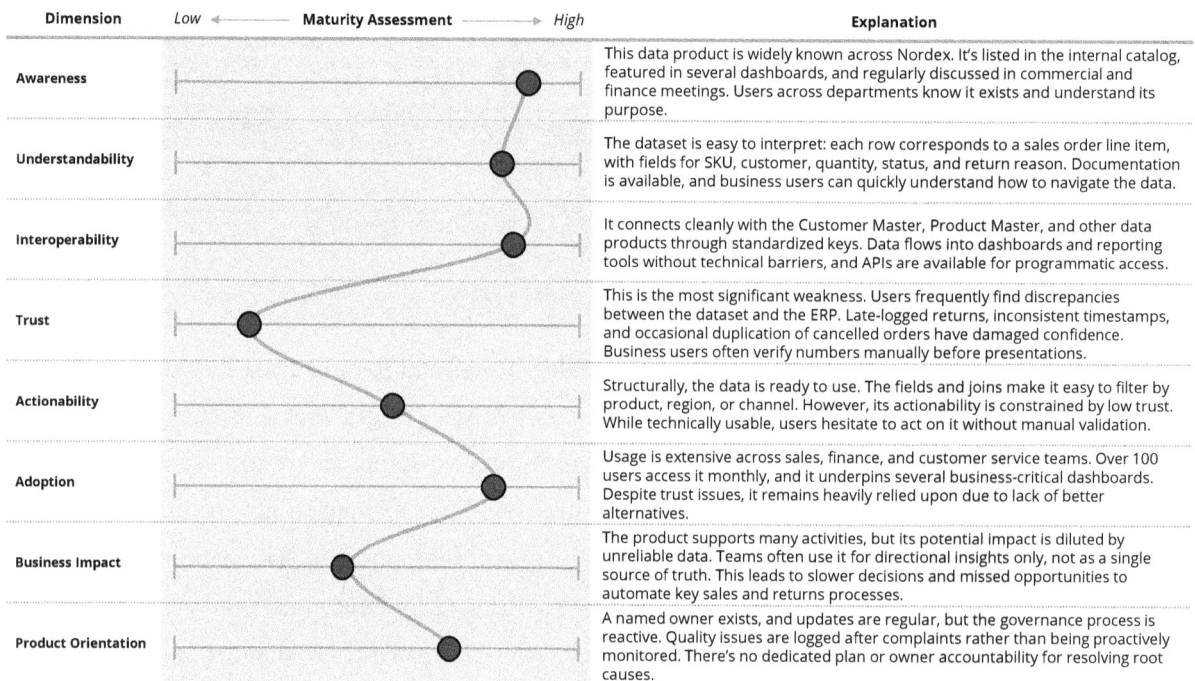

Dimension	Low ← Maturity Assessment → High	Explanation
Awareness	(high)	This data product is widely known across Nordex. It's listed in the internal catalog, featured in several dashboards, and regularly discussed in commercial and finance meetings. Users across departments know it exists and understand its purpose.
Understandability	(high)	The dataset is easy to interpret: each row corresponds to a sales order line item, with fields for SKU, customer, quantity, status, and return reason. Documentation is available, and business users can quickly understand how to navigate the data.
Interoperability	(high)	It connects cleanly with the Customer Master, Product Master, and other data products through standardized keys. Data flows into dashboards and reporting tools without technical barriers, and APIs are available for programmatic access.
Trust	(low)	This is the most significant weakness. Users frequently find discrepancies between the dataset and the ERP. Late-logged returns, inconsistent timestamps, and occasional duplication of cancelled orders have damaged confidence. Business users often verify numbers manually before presentations.
Actionability	(medium)	Structurally, the data is ready to use. The fields and joins make it easy to filter by product, region, or channel. However, its actionability is constrained by low trust. While technically usable, users hesitate to act on it without manual validation.
Adoption	(high)	Usage is extensive across sales, finance, and customer service teams. Over 100 users access it monthly, and it underpins several business-critical dashboards. Despite trust issues, it remains heavily relied upon due to lack of better alternatives.
Business Impact	(low-medium)	The product supports many activities, but its potential impact is diluted by unreliable data. Teams often use it for directional insights only, not as a single source of truth. This leads to slower decisions and missed opportunities to automate key sales and returns processes.
Product Orientation	(medium)	A named owner exists, and updates are regular, but the governance process is reactive. Quality issues are logged after complaints rather than being proactively monitored. There's no dedicated plan or owner accountability for resolving root causes.

Figure 26 – Maturity assessment of the Sales Orders and Returns data product.

These maturity assessments are useful at the individual data product level, helping you pinpoint exactly what's working and what isn't, and where to act next. But when you repeat this exercise across an entire portfolio, and if you evaluate ten or more data products in the same way, clear organizational patterns may emerge. If most products score low on a particular dimension, this might not be a coincidence, but rather reflects a broader, company-wide capability gap. The good news here is that these insights are highly actionable. They can directly inform what to prioritize next at an enterprise level to raise the overall maturity of all data products.

Here are some examples of how that can play out across the dimensions:

- **Awareness**: Low awareness often means teams don't know what data products exist or how to access them. Strengthen communication through a central data catalog, internal showcases, and training sessions. Make data products part of onboarding and data literacy programs so they're visible from day one.

- **Understandability**: When users struggle to make sense of the data, focus on improving documentation and consistency. Invest in a shared business glossary, enforce naming conventions, and include examples or "how-to" guides within each data product entry.

- **Interoperability**: Gaps here usually stem from disconnected systems or inconsistent data definitions. Reinforce shared identifiers, adopt common data models, and create enterprise integration patterns so products connect seamlessly.

- **Trust**: If users don't trust the data, implementing a data quality framework, automated validation checks, and a process for issue remediation can help. Embedding stewardship roles in key domains can also strengthen accountability.

- **Actionability**: When data products require heavy cleanup or transformation before use, it could help to embed readiness criteria into your release process. Define what "fit-for-purpose" means in your organization and certify products that meet those standards before publishing.

- **Adoption**: Adoption is often a trailing dimension where low scores here usually reflect issues across the other dimensions. Still, running a data user empowerment survey can help identify adoption barriers. Invest in training, highlight success stories, and integrate products directly into workflows so they become part of daily decision-making.

- **Business Impact**: If the impact is unclear (especially when adoption is high), you can introduce a data value ROI or quantification framework. This can help data product teams define measurable outcomes, track usage metrics, and link data initiatives directly to revenue, cost, or risk improvements.

- **Product Orientation**: Low scores here often mean data products are treated as static datasets rather than living assets. You can introduce clear ownership models, product lifecycle management, and continuous improvement cycles so data products evolve with user needs. You bring all of these things together in a data product owner activation program to train and empower data product owners.

We've now moved from looking at individual data products to spotting patterns across an entire portfolio, and started touching on what can be done at an enterprise level to raise overall performance. That naturally leads us to the next step. The next subsection takes a broader view, examining the organization's maturity: how ready it is to design, govern, and continuously improve data products at scale.

3.3.2. Maturity Framework for the Organization

In the previous section, we focused on how to measure the maturity of individual data products, and how well each one performs, how it's used, and where it can improve. Just as important is the organization's maturity: its ability to consistently build, maintain, and grow data products across teams and business units. Even the best-designed data products will struggle in an immature environment, and truly great data products rarely appear by chance. They need to be nurtured. They need the right environment, with the right people, processes, and support systems to even come into existence. Without that foundation, it's difficult for data products to be conceived, developed, or sustained in a meaningful way.

In Figure 27 below, you can see the full organizational data product maturity framework. It captures five key dimensions that together define how well an organization is set up to deliver on its data product ambitions. In the following pages, we'll unpack each of these dimensions and describe what maturity looks like at different stages.

Maturity Level	Level 1: Ad Hoc	Level 2: Initial	Level 3: Managed	Level 4: Optimized
Strategy and Vision	There is no clear data product strategy or vision. Efforts are reactive, fragmented, and driven by individual projects or departments. Leadership treats data initiatives as technical exercises rather than strategic enablers. There is little to no alignment between business goals and data product development.	Some recognition emerges that data products can create business value. Early champions or departments begin defining goals, but the vision remains localized and inconsistent. A few products are mentioned in strategic discussions, but there's no enterprise-wide roadmap or alignment across teams.	A clear data product vision is documented and linked to enterprise data and business strategy. Leadership understands how data products enable outcomes, and a formal roadmap guides priorities. A data product council or steering committee coordinates across domains, and investment planning has started to become structured.	The organization treats data products as strategic business assets. The data product strategy is fully integrated into enterprise planning, funding, and performance management. Leadership routinely reviews portfolio outcomes, aligns investments with strategic priorities, and measures success based on business impact. Data product principles are embedded in how the organization defines, builds, and delivers value.
People and Talent	There are no formal data product roles or accountabilities. Work happens on a best-effort basis, often by whoever has the time or technical know-how. Responsibilities for ownership, quality, or stewardship are unclear, and data product skills are scattered or nonexistent. Success depends mostly on individual initiative rather than a structured team setup.	Some awareness of data product roles exists, but practices are inconsistent. A few individuals act as informal owners or stewards, usually without formal recognition or dedicated time. Training is limited, and collaboration between business and data teams occurs occasionally but without standard routines or expectations.	Data product roles and responsibilities are clearly defined and staffed. Product owners and stewards have recognized accountability, and teams receive targeted training. Collaboration between business, analytics, and IT is routine, and an early community of practice or internal knowledge-sharing structure is in place.	The organization actively invests in data product talent and culture. Ownership and stewardship are built into job descriptions and career paths. Continuous training, certification, and mentorship are in place. Data product roles are fully recognized across functions, and collaboration, learning, and recognition of success are embedded in the company culture.
Process and Governance	There are no formal processes or governance structures for data products. Work happens on a project-by-project basis with no consistency or documentation. Policies for data quality, privacy, and lifecycle management are either missing or ignored. Accountability is unclear, and decisions are made reactively.	Some processes begin to take shape, usually driven by compliance or individual teams. Governance is informal and varies across domains. A few policies exist, but they are applied inconsistently. Data quality checks or reviews happen occasionally but are manual and dependent on individual diligence.	Standard processes exist for designing, certifying, and maintaining data products. A formal governance framework connects business, IT, and analytics. Policies for quality, privacy, and lifecycle management are documented and enforced. Data quality, metadata, and ownership are tracked, and a review board or steering committee oversees key decisions.	Governance and process management are embedded into daily operations and largely automated. Data products follow a clear, end-to-end lifecycle from ideation to retirement. Controls such as quality validation, lineage, and certification are enforced "as code." Portfolio reviews, ROI tracking, and risk management are systematic, and continuous improvement is built into every product's lifecycle.

Maturity Level	Level 1: Ad Hoc	Level 2: Initial	Level 3: Managed	Level 4: Optimized
Technology	The organization relies on disconnected systems and manual data handling. There is no unified data platform or shared tooling for building or consuming data products. Integration between systems is minimal, and metadata or lineage tracking is nonexistent. Most data access happens through ad hoc extracts or spreadsheets.	Some foundational technology investments have been made, such as a cloud platform or data warehouse, but usage remains siloed. Data products are created inconsistently across tools and environments. There's limited automation, and interoperability depends on individual effort. A basic catalog or repository may exist but is incomplete.	A modern data platform supports standardized data product development and sharing. Core capabilities like metadata management, lineage tracking, and role-based access are in place. Automation through CI/CD and infrastructure-as-code is established. Self-service access and secure data sharing are available, though not yet enterprise-wide.	The technology environment fully enables scalable, secure, and automated data product delivery. All data products are discoverable through a unified catalog or marketplace. Interoperability is achieved through shared schemas and identifiers. Monitoring, observability, and governance are embedded into pipelines. Reusable templates, APIs, and automation allow rapid deployment and management of hundreds of products with minimal manual effort.
Adoption	Data products exist but are rarely used. Most business decisions rely on manual reports or offline data sources. There is no visibility into who uses which data products, and no measurement of value or outcomes. Users often don't trust or even know about available data products.	Some awareness and usage begin to emerge, typically within specific teams or projects. Adoption depends on personal relationships or individual champions. Business value is discussed but not measured. Data products may be referenced in dashboards or analyses but are not embedded in regular workflows.	Adoption and usage are actively tracked through metrics and monitoring. Key business functions use data products in their daily decision-making. Feedback loops are in place to capture user satisfaction and improvement ideas. Business impact is occasionally measured through case studies or performance metrics, and success stories are shared across teams.	Data products are widely adopted, trusted, and central to how the business operates. Users across functions rely on them daily for decisions, automation, and innovation. Value creation is systematically measured using a data ROI or quantification framework. Insights from adoption data directly guide product improvement and prioritization. High adoption and proven impact continuously reinforce investment and organizational commitment.

Figure 27 – Organizational Maturity Framework for Data Products, showing maturity levels across five core dimensions.

Before diving into those dimensions, let us understand the four maturity levels themselves:

- At the **Ad Hoc** level, there is little to no maturity. Whatever efforts exist are isolated, inconsistent, and depend entirely on individual initiative or one-off projects.

- At the **Initial** level, you can start to see maturity developing in certain pockets of the organization. Specific teams, technologies, or business areas are beginning to make progress, but efforts remain uncoordinated and inconsistent.

- The **Managed** level represents a strong, stable state. At this point, data product practices are well-established across the organization, with clear roles, processes, and supporting technology. This is where many organizations should aim to be, because it provides generally decent structure and governance across critical data products, while moving toward the Optimized level often requires much higher investment that is not always worth it.

- At the **Optimized** level, data products are part of the organization's DNA. Leading companies at this stage use data products as an integral driver of business value, continuously improving and scaling their capabilities through automation, feedback loops, and a deeply embedded data culture.

3.3.2.1. Strategy and Vision

A strong data product strategy starts with a clear connection to the organization's broader business strategy. Data products are not a goal in and of themselves. Just like any other technical capability or governance initiative, they only exist to help the organization achieve its business objectives. That means the organization must have a clearly articulated view of how data products enable its strategic priorities: how they contribute to efficiency, growth, customer experience, innovation, or whatever the enterprise is truly trying to achieve.

There needs to be an explicit articulation of this connection. A mature organization can clearly answer questions such as: Why do we need data products? How exactly will they help us deliver on our business goals? Which strategic outcomes depend on them? Without that clarity, it is easy to fall into the trap of building data products for their own sake, producing more noise than impact.

A good example of this comes from a large manufacturing company I worked with. The company had been trying to strengthen its data management and governance capabilities, but quickly realized it was impossible to govern all data across the enterprise to the same standard. It would have been too expensive, too broad, and too slow. So instead, they reframed their data strategy entirely around data products. They decided that data products would be the way to deliver governance, quality, and access control where it mattered most. Through data products, they could apply the right levels of data quality, metadata, and access control to the datasets that actually drove value. This approach became part of their formal enterprise data strategy. It was shared broadly through internal learning sessions, published in the company's internal wiki, and communicated to all business and technology teams. Everyone in the company could refer back to it and see how their work connected to the broader vision.

At **low maturity**, none of this exists. There might be people talking about "data products" or "data as an asset," but there is no clear explanation of why they matter or how they fit into the company's strategy. Efforts are ad hoc and reactive, and each team defines "data product" differently. There's little leadership alignment, and no one can point to a shared document or statement that connects data products to business outcomes.

At **high maturity**, the organization has a well-documented, enterprise-level data product strategy that directly links to the overall business vision. Senior leadership not only understands this connection but also actively champions it. Every major initiative identifies the data products required to support it, and these products are planned, funded, and tracked as part of the organization's core business strategy. The organization treats data products as strategic business assets rather than technical outputs. The data product strategy is fully integrated into enterprise planning, budgeting, and performance management. Leadership routinely reviews data product portfolios, evaluates their outcomes, and ensures investments remain aligned with strategic priorities. Success is measured not just by delivery milestones but by tangible business impact. Data product principles are embedded in how the organization defines, builds, and delivers value, shaping both its operating model and its culture. Over time, this creates a self-sustaining cycle where business strategy drives data product priorities, and those data products, in turn, enable the business to execute its strategy more effectively.

Best practices for driving maturity in Strategy and Vision include:

- **Explicitly articulating and publishing the strategy:** Do not assume that because leadership has discussed it, others know it exists. Write it down, publish it, and make it accessible to everyone.

- **Leveraging existing knowledge:** There is a rich body of public knowledge explaining why data products are valuable, and how they simplify architecture, enable data mesh principles, and accelerate use cases. Use that as a foundation and tailor it to your context.

- **Engaging business stakeholders early and visibly:** The true test of a successful data product strategy is when business leaders (specifically outside data or IT teams) say, "This made a difference." That alignment can only happen if you bring them in from the start. Do so radically.

3.3.2.2. People and Talent

No data product strategy can succeed without the right people. Even the most advanced frameworks, architectures, or tools will fall short if the human element isn't there to bring them to life. At the end of the day, even in a world that's becoming increasingly automated and technology-enabled, organizations still depend on people, including their skills, their mindset, and their ability to collaborate effectively.

The People and Talent dimension looks at whether an organization has both the right capabilities and the right structures to enable those capabilities to thrive. On one hand, it's about talent, and whether the organization has people with the necessary skills to design, build, and maintain high-quality data products. This includes data product managers with a product-oriented mindset, engineers who understand modular design and interoperability, and governance professionals who ensure standards and stewardship are applied consistently.

On the other hand, this dimension is about enablement, and how people are empowered to work effectively and grow in their roles. That means having clearly defined roles and responsibilities, such as what it means to be a data product owner or a data steward, and ensuring everyone understands how decisions are made and how accountability is shared across business and technical functions. It's not just about assigning roles, but also about continuously developing the people behind them. Mature organizations invest in training, mentorship, and communities of practice that make talent development part of everyday work, enabling individuals to continue expanding their skills while collaborating more effectively. When these elements come together—skilled people supported by clear structures, shared accountability, and a culture that values collaboration and learning—data products can truly thrive.

The vast majority of organizations have a **low maturity** in People and Talent. People may know the buzzword "data product," but when you look closer, there's very little structure behind it. There are no formal roles or accountabilities in place, and work tends to happen on a best-effort basis, usually driven by whoever has the time, the technical know-how, or the loudest request. Responsibilities for ownership, quality, or stewardship are unclear, and teams often operate independently without shared standards or alignment. What's interesting is that the raw talent is usually there. Many organizations already have skilled people, such as business analysts, data engineers, and other roles, who collectively have the right ingredients to make data products work. But that talent isn't being brought together, nurtured, or guided. There's no dedicated training, no formal data product roles, and no clear expectations for how people should collaborate or who is accountable for what. As a result, success depends almost entirely on individual initiative rather than on a repeatable, structured setup.

At **high maturity**, things look very different. The organization has built a strong foundation of clearly defined roles, teamwork, and ongoing learning. Data product ownership and stewardship are no longer side tasks but part of official job descriptions and performance expectations. Everyone knows who does what and how their work connects to the bigger picture. Teams are cross-functional and steady, bringing together business experts, engineers, analysts, and governance specialists who focus on shared outcomes instead of working in silos.

Training and growth are built into daily work. Data product owners and engineers have access to real learning opportunities, mentorship, and clear career paths. Communities of practice help people share templates, lessons, and ideas across teams, so knowledge doesn't get stuck. Leadership invests in all this because they know talent is what really makes or breaks success. In Figure 28, you can see an example of a job description for a data product owner, showing how responsibilities and expectations are made official and visible to everyone.

That said, you have to keep things realistic. If your company has thousands of employees and a big data team, all of this makes perfect sense. But if you have a small IT department with ten people, it doesn't make sense to build a "community of practice" when the whole community is basically two people. The point isn't to copy the structure of large enterprises but to apply the same logic at your own scale. You still need clarity about who owns what, you still need people to learn and grow, but you don't need layers of process to get there.

Job Description – Data Product Owner

Data Product Owner	
Department	Enterprise Data & Analytics Office
Reporting Hierarchy	Head of Data Analytics and Enablement
Work Location	Chicago, IL

Job Overview
NorthShield Insurance Group is a mid-sized insurance provider specializing in personal and commercial coverage across the U.S. We're on a mission to modernize how data supports every part of our business. As the Data Product Owner – Claims & Policy Data, you will own the end-to-end lifecycle of data products related to claims and policy information. Your goal is to ensure these data products are accurate, reliable, easy to use, and directly enable key business priorities such as customer experience, fraud detection, and operational efficiency. You'll translate business needs into data product capabilities, coordinate with engineering and governance teams, and make sure that what we build delivers measurable value to the organization.

Responsibilities

- Act as the single point of accountability for the Claims & Policy Data Product.
- Define and maintain the vision, roadmap, and success criteria for the data product.
- Work closely with business stakeholders (e.g., Claims Operations, Underwriting, Finance) to understand data needs and translate them into product features.
- Collaborate with data engineers, modelers, and quality specialists to ensure the data is accurate, timely, and well-documented.
- Manage and prioritize the product backlog, balancing business value, technical debt, and compliance requirements.
- Ensure metadata, lineage, and data quality metrics are captured and visible in the enterprise catalog.
- Coordinate with governance and compliance teams to align with privacy, security, and regulatory standards.
- Track usage, adoption, and impact metrics to continuously improve the product.

Skills and Qualifications

- ✓ 5+ years of experience in data management, business analysis, or analytics.
- ✓ Strong understanding of data governance principles and data lifecycle management.
- ✓ Familiarity with modern data platforms (e.g., Snowflake, Databricks, AWS, or GCP).
- ✓ Proven ability to work with cross-functional teams (IT, business, analytics).
- ✓ Comfortable using tools like Jira, Confluence, or similar for backlog and documentation management.
- ✓ Excellent communication skills and ability to translate technical details into business language.
- ✓ Background in insurance or financial services is a plus.

Figure 28 – Example job description for a Data Product Owner, illustrating how responsibilities, skills, and organizational context can be clearly defined to support effective data product management.

What matters most is that people understand their roles, take ownership, and feel supported to keep improving. When that happens, you end up with a culture where trusted, high-quality data products can grow naturally.

Best practices for driving maturity in People and Talent include:

- **Formalizing roles and accountabilities**: Don't skip this step. Clearly define what it means to be a data product owner, steward, or engineer, and capture it in a RACI matrix. With today's generative AI tools, building such matrices and role definitions is faster and easier than ever. Don't assume people share the same understanding just because you've explained it once; document it, publish it, and make sure everyone can reference it.

- **Contextualizing talent development to your organization**: Think about your specific technology and business environment. For example, if your enterprise data platform is Snowflake, include it in your enablement plan. Ensure your data product managers, engineers, and stewards are fluent in the platforms and tools that matter most to you. While many data product skills are transferable, technology evolves quickly, and being hands-on and current within your own stack is key.

- **Defining and celebrating growth**: Be explicit about what "great" looks like. Establish clear development metrics, recognize success stories, and invest time in helping people see their impact. Building and managing data products should feel exciting and rewarding, not like a back-office chore. Celebrate collaboration and impact to make data work something people are proud of.

3.3.2.3. Process and Governance

Process and governance ensure the organization has a consistent, structured way to manage how data products are designed, built, and maintained. You want the people we talked about in the previous section, your data product owners, stewards, engineers, and analysts, to have clear guidance and repeatable ways of working so they don't have to reinvent the wheel every time. This is where we fight our mortal enemies: tribal knowledge, inconsistency, and duplicate effort. Without solid processes, every team ends up doing things their own way, which leads to confusion and rework. The goal here is to help people learn from what's already been done, improve it, and scale success.

Depending on the data product, its contents, and the use cases it enables, Process and Governance can also involve risk management and quality assurance. The right governance ensures that data products are compliant, traceable, and safe to use. For example, imagine a healthcare provider that built a "Patient 360" data product to combine patient records, treatment outcomes, and care interactions across clinics. Without strong governance, such a data product could easily expose sensitive patient information and violate HIPAA and GDPR privacy laws. A missing access control, a poorly designed data-sharing rule, or an undocumented transformation could lead to fines, loss of trust, or even a full shutdown of operations. In cases like this, having the right governance framework in place isn't just good practice; it's existential.

At the same time, we need to avoid falling into the classic trap of making governance a heavy bureaucracy. Data governance has a terrible reputation for being slow, full of red tape, and painfully expensive. This is to be avoided. This dimension is about finding the right balance: giving people enough structure and clarity to work efficiently, without so much control that you choke creativity and momentum.

Earlier in Chapter 2: Designing and Building Great Data Products, we already discussed key building blocks such as the data product lifecycle, value quantification, how to build a business case, data product blueprints, and certification criteria. The Process and Governance dimension is essentially about putting those things into motion and embedding them into clear processes, documented steps, and practical governance practices.

Taking all of that and applying it to a **low-maturity** environment, you typically find there's simply no process and no real governance around data products. There's no defined lifecycle, no certification criteria, and no documented steps for managing data products end to end, neither at the enterprise level nor within individual teams. In my experience, this is very common, even in large and otherwise sophisticated organizations. There are often general data policies, standards, or process documents at some level in the company, but they rarely make it all the way into how data products are actually built, maintained, and governed in practice. Despite a fairly rich body of knowledge on how to do so, few organizations have consistently applied it to data products.

At **high maturity**, governance is fully integrated into daily operations. Processes for certifying, maintaining, and retiring data products are standardized and automated wherever possible. Data quality, lineage, and compliance checks run "as code" within pipelines. Portfolio reviews, ROI tracking, and risk management are part of the regular business rhythm. Governance committees operate not as gatekeepers but as enablers, ensuring that decisions are consistent, transparent, and fast. In these organizations, governance becomes invisible; it's simply how work gets done.

Best practices for driving maturity in Process and Governance include:

- **Designing governance to enable, not restrict:** Build processes that help teams move faster with confidence rather than slow them down. Put some deliberate attention into this. For example, measure how long key governance decisions take and how many approvals are involved, or run quick pulse surveys to gather feedback on specific parts of your end-to-end data product lifecycle. These are simple yet powerful ways to ensure your governance is truly enabling, not suffocating.

- **Automating wherever possible:** Embed controls such as quality validation, lineage, and certification directly into pipelines and workflows. The less governance depends on manual effort, the more consistently and efficiently it will be applied. Automation ensures compliance happens in the background, not as a separate bureaucratic step.

- **Creating reusable governance assets:** As described earlier in Chapter 2 of this book, organizations should define reusable components, such as a standardized data product lifecycle, certification criteria, and review checklists. Make these assets easy to find and reference. Publish them in a discoverable internal wiki or playbook so teams can apply them consistently without reinventing the process each time.

3.3.2.4. Technology

In this part of the framework, we focus on the technology dimension, which is the set of capabilities that allow a data product organization to actually function and scale. The goal of the book here isn't to provide a deep technical blueprint or tool comparison. There are already countless books, blogs, and vendor materials that cover those topics in great detail. We want to highlight the kinds of technological components that tend to exist in thriving data product organizations and how they enable consistency, speed, and quality.

Typically, there are a few core building blocks that define a strong technology foundation. First is the data platform itself. This is a modern, usually cloud-based environment that enables the design, storage, and processing of data products efficiently. A metadata management capability can ensure that data products carry context about where the data comes from, what it means, and who owns it. That's often achieved through integrated metadata catalogs and lineage tracking tools. Then there's automation and observability, which are critical for maintaining reliability at scale. Mature organizations embed automation into pipelines, using infrastructure-as-code and CI/CD practices to eliminate manual deployment bottlenecks. Interoperability technology ensures that data products can connect and work together seamlessly through shared schemas, identifiers, and APIs.

Together, these capabilities form the technical backbone of a high-performing data product ecosystem. However, they should not exist as isolated or one-off investments. True maturity comes from coherence across the entire technology landscape, where each capability fits together as part of an intentional design. The data platform should naturally integrate with the catalog, automation pipelines should feed metadata, and APIs should be built on shared standards that promote consistency and reuse. Indeed, the goal is not to have the most advanced tool in every category, but to ensure that all components work together to a minimally required level of maturity.

In this regard, there are real, strategic choices to be made. Some companies choose to fully commit to a single ecosystem, for example, building everything within Google Cloud. This approach simplifies integration, governance, and security, as everything operates under a single vendor's architecture and standards. It can accelerate delivery and reduce friction between tools, but it also introduces a form of dependency: once you commit, it becomes difficult and costly to change direction later. Other organizations take the opposite approach, deliberately maintaining flexibility and avoiding vendor lock-in. They may combine different tools and cloud providers, selecting the best solution for each need. This gives them more control and resilience, but also requires stronger internal governance and architectural discipline to keep everything working together. Neither model is inherently better; rather, what matters is that you understand the tradeoffs and make a deliberate choice.

At **low maturity**, the technology landscape is usually fragmented and inconsistent. Different teams use their own tools, platforms, and scripts, often without any shared standards or integration. Data pipelines are manually maintained, with minimal or no automation. Metadata is scattered or missing, making it hard to understand where data comes from or how it's being used. There is no single place to find or access data products, and reliability depends heavily on individual effort rather than a stable technical foundation.

At **high maturity**, the organization operates on a unified and well-integrated technology backbone. The platform, catalog, automation, and interoperability layers work together seamlessly, supporting consistency and scalability. Data pipelines are automated, metadata is captured by design, and data products are easily discoverable and shareable through governed access. Technology choices are intentional and coordinated, reducing duplication and technical debt. Teams can focus on delivering value rather than maintaining infrastructure, because the ecosystem itself is built to support speed, trust, and long-term sustainability.

Best practices for driving maturity in Technology include:

- **Automating the connective tissue:** Interoperability, metadata, and observability are what tie your data ecosystem together. Build them into your architecture by design—shared identifiers, embedded lineage tracking, and built-in monitoring. If teams have to manually document or validate every connection, you've already lost efficiency. Automation here is what keeps the system alive and coherent.

- **Automating everything repeatable:** Use infrastructure-as-code, CI/CD, and workflow automation to remove manual bottlenecks. Automate not just pipelines but also testing, monitoring, and certification.

- **Deliberately choosing your architectural stance:** Decide consciously whether to go all-in on a single ecosystem (like AWS, Azure, or GCP) or to maintain a multi-cloud or hybrid setup. Both can work, but only if the choice is strategic and supported by clear governance.

- **Enabling flexibility through structured freedom**: Define just enough structure to keep things coherent, like shared standards, automated access, and built-in compliance, and then get out of the way. The best architectures are the ones that make doing the right thing the easiest thing.

3.3.2.5. Adoption

The Adoption dimension measures how widely data products are used within the organization. It looks at whether people know they exist, trust them, and rely on them in their daily work. Strong adoption means data products have become part of everyday operations and decisions.

Most maturity frameworks focus on whether the right capabilities exist, but often overlook adoption. As I explained in my article "Data maturity models—Why having the capabilities in place isn't enough," adoption is what proves that the rest of the framework is working. Adoption trails the other dimensions because it depends on them being in place first, and it's also the one that ultimately shows if data products are delivering real value.[2]

At **low maturity**, data products don't exist at all, or if they do, they're isolated, inconsistent, and lack any real evidence of adoption or impact (which, technically, as per our discussion of key properties of data products in Section 1.2. Key Properties of Data Products, disqualifies them from being data products). At slightly higher maturity, some awareness begins to form. A few teams may start using data products for specific needs, but adoption is still uneven and depends heavily on individual champions. There's limited measurement of value, and usage tends to fade once those individuals move on or priorities shift.

At **high maturity**, adoption and impact are unmistakable. Data products are part of everyday business, used naturally across teams without people even thinking about it. Decisions, operations, and innovation all rely on them. The business can clearly point to where and how data products drive value, and new initiatives are designed with data products woven in from the start.

Best practices for driving maturity in Adoption include:

- **Making adoption visible:** Track and communicate usage metrics, such as how many users access a product, how often it's used, or which business processes depend on it. Visibility turns adoption into a tangible, shared success and helps teams see the value of what they've built.

- **Designing with users, not just for them:** Bring business users into the process early. Let them help define requirements, validate prototypes, and shape how products are delivered. Co-creation builds trust and ensures that what's developed fits real needs, making adoption natural rather than forced.

---

[2] See (Koenders, Data maturity models — Why having the capabilities in place isn't enough, 2024).

- **Assigning ownership for adoption:** Treat adoption as a core responsibility, not an afterthought. Data product owners should be accountable for driving awareness, enabling users, and tracking engagement. Their job isn't finished at launch; it's to make sure the product actually lands and delivers impact.

3.4. Organizational Change Journey

Building successful data products in an enterprise requires more than technical capabilities – it requires organizational change. This chapter focuses on the broader change journey rather than just product-level maturity. We introduce John Kotter's famous 8-Step Change Model as a guide for leaders driving a data-product shift. Kotter's approach helps translate the challenge of "becoming data-product-driven" into concrete actions and milestones across the organization.

By now, we've covered a lot of ground. We unpacked what a data product actually is and what properties ensure that some data products succeed where others fail. We explored the architectural blueprints that make data products work, and how to manage them across a portfolio. We looked at how to measure the maturity of individual data products and then scaled that perspective to assess the organization's maturity as a whole.

But across everything we discussed, for many data leaders, the questions then become: How do all these pieces come together in practice? How do you start this journey? Where do you begin, how do you build momentum, and how do you sustain it over time? This is what the broader organizational journey is about: turning the concepts and frameworks we've discussed into a structured path for change and real, visible progress.

This topic is especially relevant for people in leadership roles such as Chief Data Officers, Heads of Data Enablement, or Data and Analytics Directors. They may sit on the business or technology side and are the people tasked with driving cultural and operational change across the enterprise.

I have spent close to 15 years helping some of the world's most data-driven organizations move through this kind of transformation, integrating data as a true asset and embedding data products into their operating models. I have seen this up close across Europe, the United States, Latin

America, and Asia, and across industries like insurance, banking, medical technology, manufacturing, and the public sector. While every organization's journey is unique, certain patterns repeat themselves. There are common paths that work and others that reliably do not. Often, my teams are brought in precisely when something was tried before and failed, which gives us a clear view of what helps organizations truly evolve and what holds them back.

There is naturally some correlation between this journey and the organizational maturity framework discussed in the previous chapter. In practice, as you move through these phases, you're effectively progressing from a low level of maturity toward a more consistent, enterprise-wide capability. The difference here is that this section focuses less on how to measure maturity, but rather on how change as a process.

3.4.1. John Kotter and the 8-Step Change Model

John P. Kotter is a Harvard Business School professor and a pioneer in change management. In his landmark book Leading Change (Kotter, Leading Change, 1996) and an influential 1995 Harvard Business Review article (Kotter, 1995), Kotter distilled his observations from about 100 organizations undergoing major transformations. He identified and extracted the common success factors from decades of research and documented them as eight steps toward successful change. Kotter's model sequences the critical actions from generating buy-in through embedding new habits, based on a real-world study.

Over time, Kotter's eight-step model has become one of the most commonly used frameworks for driving large-scale change. It's appreciated for its clarity and for giving leaders a structured sequence of steps; the original eight steps remain widely used and practical. For our purposes, the structure is helpful because it mirrors many of the phases involved in building a data product culture, from creating a shared vision to embedding new behaviors into day-to-day operations.

Kotter's framework lays out a structured path for guiding an organization through complex change. It starts with creating shared urgency and alignment, then builds momentum by engaging others, removing blockers, and showing quick wins. Over time, it shifts into maintaining progress and making new behaviors part of the culture. These eight steps, shown in Figure 29, offer a practical lens for understanding how to move from early enthusiasm to lasting change. In the rest of this chapter, we'll walk through each step and show how it can be applied to the organizational journey of adopting and scaling data products.

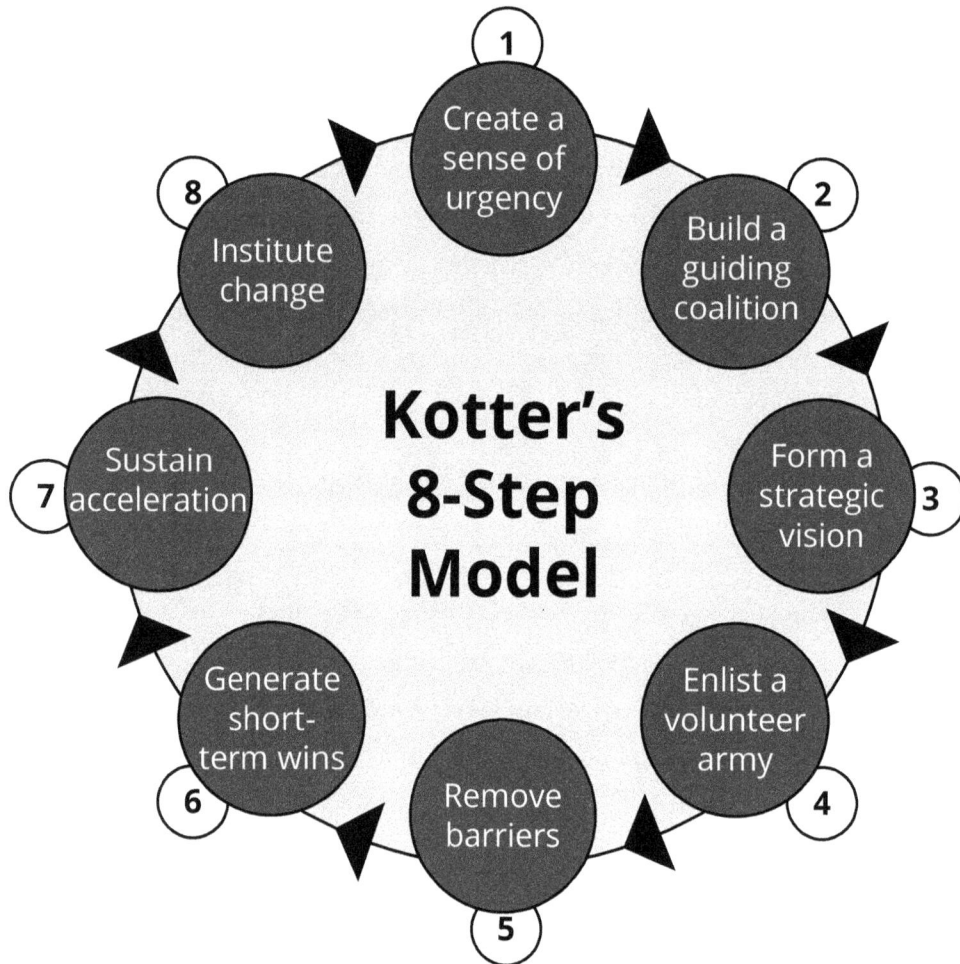

Figure 29 – Visual summary of Kotter's 8-Step Model for leading organizational change, as originally introduced in (Kotter, 1996).

3.4.2. Step 1: Create a Sense of Urgency

Kotter's first step is to make people aware that change is needed now. He stresses using compelling data or events to show that the current situation can't continue. Leaders should identify critical opportunities or risks that demand immediate action and explain why the status quo is no longer viable.

For data products, this means telling a convincing story about why the old data approach is failing and what opportunities await with a product mindset. Leaders might highlight costly delays caused by siloed spreadsheets, missed market signals that competitors have already capitalized on, or looming regulations (such as new privacy laws or AI requirements) that current processes can't meet.

Indeed, one of the most powerful things you can do at this stage is to craft a narrative, a story you can tell over and over again that helps people see why data products matter. A good narrative takes the concept of data products and places it squarely in your organization's world. Don't stick to the textbook or generic slides. Make it specific. Use language and examples that people recognize, and tie them to something that genuinely matters in your business. The point is not to sell hype, but to make the idea feel real and relevant.

In one large pharmaceutical company I worked with, researchers were running hundreds of experiments across different labs, each keeping their own notes. These notes were often stored inconsistently, sometimes on local drives, sometimes in lab notebooks, and sometimes not at all. A lot of incredibly valuable insight, especially from failed experiments, was effectively lost forever. In the past, scientists were not interested in spending time documenting or sharing information about experiments that had already failed. It was tedious, time-consuming, and pulled them away from what they cared about most: designing and running new experiments. Over time, that created real fatigue and a bad taste for anything related to structured data management.

When we came in, we didn't start with a platform or a new technology. We started by crafting a story. We asked, what if all of those handwritten notes and experiment logs could be transformed into a living knowledge base for future research? What if scientists could record their findings in whatever format they preferred, and language models could automatically, safely, securely, and cost-effectively process and extract structured information? That information could then feed a reusable "experiment data product" that future teams could query to see what had worked, what had failed, and why.

Today, many pharmaceutical companies are using artificial intelligence to simulate experiments before running them in the lab. These models can test thousands of possibilities and identify which approaches are most likely to succeed. But to do that well, they need large, high-quality datasets that reflect what has already been tried, what worked, and what did not. That is exactly what this kind of reusable experiment data product provides. It enables AI systems to learn from the organization's collective research history, improving accuracy, reducing costs, and accelerating discovery. The result is not just more efficient experimentation, but better-informed science and, ultimately, the ability to create better medicines faster.

All of a sudden, you have a story that ties data products to something much larger. It connects to innovation, the company's mission, and even to real people who will benefit from better, faster treatments. The narrative gave scientists a sense of possibility without demanding more of their time. It also gave leadership a hint of a vision of how smarter data reuse could accelerate innovation and reduce wasted effort. In the end, we hadn't built anything yet, but the story itself changed the conversation. It created belief.

3.4.3. Step 2: Build a Guiding Coalition

The second step is to put together a strong team that can drive the change. Kotter advises forming a coalition of committed people across the organization, including leaders with authority and employees with influence. This guiding coalition coordinates the effort, makes key decisions, and helps overcome resistance. It's a volunteer leadership network that champions the change.

In the context of a data product transformation, this coalition is about shaping the vision, securing support, and keeping momentum alive when things get hard. What this coalition looks like can vary dramatically depending on your organization. If you're in a young, fast-moving company with a start-up mentality where cross-functional collaboration is already part of the culture, the coalition might be relatively informal, made up of senior engineers, a business general manager, and a product-minded executive. But if you're in a century-old company with tens of thousands of employees and well-established silos, this coalition may look a bit different, requiring a more deliberate approach.

In either case, the coalition needs to start with a data leader of sorts: someone who believes in the value of data products and is willing to fight for them. This person can sit on either the business or technology side. I've seen both work. What's critical is that they have authority, credibility, and staying power. They must be able to champion the change across silos and have the respect of their peers. And perhaps most importantly, this leader needs to be convincing. They need to be able to tell the story. The next step in the change process that we'll get to in the next section is about crafting a vision, but the truth is that plenty of people have a decent vision in their heads—they just fail to communicate it. Especially when it comes to data products, where many of the individual pieces aren't necessarily new, the real difference comes from how you frame it: how you bring those pieces together in a new configuration, how you explain the value, and how you get the organization to rally behind it.

You'll also need someone with at least one foot firmly in the technology organization. This isn't just about vision—it's about discipline. If you're not building with a solid architectural foundation, things can unravel quickly. You need someone who understands the importance of data modeling, lineage, quality, and security, and who can keep those concerns from being ignored in the name of speed. In some cases, this can be the same person as the data leader. If the data leader sits in IT or reports to the CIO, the technology depth may already be in place.

And then, you need the business. Many data programs begin with a well-meaning idea, good intentions, and often a vendor, but falter because they skip the single most important prerequisite for success: business traction.[3] Often, the first round of funding comes from a discretionary pot controlled by a CIO or CDO, and the hope is that the "real" business stakeholders will get on board later. But that rarely happens, and without early and meaningful business buy-in, programs stall the moment that first funding round runs out. At that point, additional resources require contributions from departmental budgets, and business leaders are (perhaps rightly) skeptical, especially if they weren't involved in shaping the initial use case.

The result? A product no one uses. A data catalog with five logins per month. A dashboard no one relies on. A quality rule that solves a problem no one actually has. Or indeed, a data product that isn't performing. I've seen it too many times to count.

But when the business is brought in early as a co-owner of the use case, you can gain clarity on what's truly needed and tie the work directly to business outcomes, ensuring the problem is real and the

---

[3] See Koenders, W. (2024, October 16). From data to decisions: Engaging stakeholders early for maximum impact.

solution will actually be adopted. And you earn the right to ask for more investment later, because you can point to real value already delivered.

Hence, to make a data product transformation stick, you need a guiding coalition: a small but credible group that believes in the opportunity and has the authority and influence to drive change. This coalition should include a data-savvy leader who can tell a compelling story, a technology anchor who ensures architectural discipline, and a business champion who sees the real-world value and is willing to co-own the problem. With the coalition in place, the next step is to align that team behind a clear, inspiring vision that frames the opportunity in a way people can understand and rally around.

3.4.4. Step 3: Form a Strategic Vision

Kotter's Step 3 is to create a clear vision to guide all activities. Kotter says the vision should describe how the future will be different and outline how initiatives link to that future. A strong vision helps people understand the change and what success looks like.

This vision should build directly on the urgency established in Step 1. In fact, let's return briefly to the pharmaceutical example introduced earlier. In Step 1, we used that story to demonstrate why the status quo was unsustainable: researchers' notes scattered across drives, insights lost forever, experiments repeated unnecessarily, and an inability to leverage AI, all of which posed a real threat of losing to the competition.

A strategic vision for that organization might begin with a clear belief:
data products will sit at the heart of the company's research and AI strategy.

Breakthrough science and responsible AI depend on the quality, completeness, and reusability of all experimental data, including failed attempts. Both patient outcomes and the company's long-term competitiveness hinge on transforming this scattered, fragile information into a durable, trustworthy asset.

In this strategic vision, every experiment contributes to a living, evolving knowledge base. Scientists can record their observations in any format (e.g., handwritten, typed, or audio), while AI automatically extracts structure and meaning. A reusable experiment data product becomes a core asset: a single, authoritative layer feeding downstream analytics, modeling, and simulation tools. AI models learn from the organization's full research history, dramatically reducing redundant experimentation and accelerating discovery.

A strategic vision should describe not only the desired future state but also what that future means for the organization in concrete terms. In our pharmaceutical example, this could include goals such as reducing the time required to prepare new studies or accelerating the discovery of new molecules by a specified percentage. Such goals help people see what "better" looks like and begin to imagine how their work could change when data products sit at the foundation of scientific research. Vision without clarity becomes abstraction; vision with defined outcomes becomes direction.

From there, the vision must connect to real initiatives that build the capabilities that make it possible. In our example, this might include defining a data operating model that defines data ownership. Someone must be accountable for ensuring that experiment notes are captured, stored, and governed correctly. Someone else might be accountable for storing and later democratizing the downstream data product.

Other initiatives might relate to the technology backbone. Many organizations find that progress accelerates when they commit to a coherent stack rather than stitching together fragmented tools. In our example, this could involve selecting a modern data platform that supports unstructured ingestion, automated metadata extraction, secure storage, and scalable AI workflows. Examples of such ecosystems are Databricks or Snowflake combined with an orchestration and catalog layer.

With the right operating model and technology foundation in place, the strategic vision shifts from aspiration to executable roadmap. And once that vision is clear, the next challenge is gathering the people who will help bring it to life, which is where Kotter's fourth step begins.

3.4.5. Step 4: Enlist a Volunteer Army

Kotter's fourth step is to build broad-based support by enlisting a large group of volunteers. Kotter writes that major change can occur only when large numbers of people rally around a common opportunity. The volunteer army spreads the vision and shares responsibility, essentially leveraging some sort of grassroots enthusiasm.

Now, I'm not entirely sure I agree with Kotter, at least, not as it relates to how this idea plays out in most data product transformations. When I hear the term "volunteer army," I picture a massive, coordinated force marching in unison toward a well-defined goal. But if I think about the successful data product change journeys I've seen, that's not really how it starts. You don't begin with an army. You have to win a few fights first before anyone is ready to rally at scale. If we stick with the military metaphor, then let's call it a targeted insertion force, not a full army just yet.

I agree with Kotter's use of the word volunteer.

That part resonates, because the opposite would be a paid-for army—people whose job is explicitly to drive this change. I've just never seen that work in the early stages of a data product transformation. You don't launch this with a fully staffed team whose only responsibility is to work on data products from day one. More often than not, the people who help get this moving are doing it alongside their existing responsibilities. They're solution architects who already think in terms of data products. They're analysts who are tired of redoing the same data prep every month. They're business leaders who are fed up with not getting the answers they need and are willing to try something new. They're not being hired into formal roles with "Data Product" in the title. They're people who see the potential and raise their hand. You're looking for people who are already doing something adjacent or who want to do something like this. That's your real volunteer army.

Once you've found that initial high-value problem that a data product can meaningfully solve, you build a focused team around it. You need someone from the business side who lives and breathes the use case, and someone from the technology side who can help you build something real without blowing up existing infrastructure. That's your starting point. You don't need a full council of data domain owners, privacy leads, or compliance stewards—not yet. While I made the case in Chapter 3.1. Data Product Teams, Roles, and Responsibilities for those broader roles, the truth is that including all of them in your initial setup will overcomplicate things. You want to make real progress, which requires focus. You don't yet build for scale, and you shouldn't overengineer governance.

Build something useful. Get someone to use it. That's your first win.
And that's what earns you the right to scale.

3.4.6. Step 5: Enable Action by Removing Barriers

In Step 5, Kotter emphasizes removing the obstacles that impede change. He advises identifying and eliminating structural or cultural barriers to empower people to take action, clearing the way for innovation.

So, let's identify the most common barriers to enabling data products. In most organizations trying to drive a data product change journey, certain structural, cultural, and operational challenges keep arising. See Figure 30 for some of the top ones I've seen, along with what you can do to address them.

Key Barrier	What You Can Do About It
Lack of ownership or accountability	There are two actions to consider. First, to clarify the *role* of a data product owner alongside its key responsibilities. Second, for an initial set of prioritized data products, you can assign *real names* and drive ownership for specific data products.
Fragmented or siloed data landscape	This might be a real constraint, but it's not one you can always solve up front. Instead, data products can be part of the solution: they offer a path to integrate or stitch data across silos in a purposeful, value-driven way. So, the action would be to see this as an opportunity to address, rather than a challenge.
Tooling and infrastructure constraints	It may help to agree on a commonly supported tooling stack, such as Databricks, Snowflake, dbt, or other platforms your team already uses. A shared foundation helps avoid wheel reinvention and makes new work easier to start.
Unclear funding and resourcing model	Data products often fall into a gap between business and IT budgets. To overcome this, you can tie early efforts to discretionary or transformation budgets, and then demonstrate sufficient value to secure co-funding from business functions. You can gradually move towards a cost-sharing model.
Cultural resistance and mindset gaps	This is the heart of most change journeys, and this entire section is dedicated to solving for it. Targeted data literacy initiatives, such as a "data product bootcamp" or executive education sessions, can help to accelerate the culture shift.

Figure 30 – Common barriers to data product adoption and practical ways to address them.

As highlighted by Kotter International (2025), many barriers to change are embedded in an organization's habits and norms. Kotter points out that even leaders themselves often recognize how their own management practices have become overly bureaucratic. These legacy processes carry tremendous staying power and often continue unchecked simply because "that's how we've always done it." Practices that may once have been useful can outlive their purpose, becoming quiet roadblocks that stall progress. Alongside this, Kotter names several other cultural and behavioral obstacles that frequently impede transformation efforts: siloed or parochial mindsets, resistance to sharing control, pressure to deliver on short-term targets, limited access to decision-makers, and the kind of risk-aversion that discourages experimentation. These are not small challenges. They are systemic in nature and often invisible at first glance. Yet if left unaddressed, they will quietly sap the energy out of any change initiative, no matter how well-designed the strategy or how compelling the business case.

To begin removing these kinds of barriers, you first have to understand them. That starts by asking better questions. Why did previous data or digital efforts stall? Were they supported at the beginning but quietly deprioritized later? Did they fail to get business buy-in or struggle with technology gaps? Were they technically sound but lacked champions with decision-making authority?

3.4.7. Step 6: Generate Short-Term Wins

Kotter's sixth step focuses on generating and celebrating short-term wins, which are those early signs of progress that validate the path of change and keep momentum alive. As described by Kotter International (2025), these "wins" serve as the molecular building blocks of broader transformation. They are the small, observable markers that show things are moving in the right direction, and they play a vital role in maintaining enthusiasm and engagement.

Wins can come in many forms: a lesson learned, a process improvement, a changed behavior, or a key stakeholder who begins to support the effort. What matters is that they help the team move closer to the opportunity and are communicated clearly and often. They should be backed by observable data that tell the story in validated, verifiable, and ideally quantifiable terms.

To truly drive impact, these wins must be relevant to the challenge at hand, resonate with others beyond those directly involved, and be concrete enough that others can learn from them or replicate them elsewhere. This turns individual wins into shared accelerants of change.

The most meaningful type of quick win in a data product–driven change journey is clear progress toward an actual data product. That could mean anything from getting a product scoped and designed, to standing up an MVP version and putting it in the hands of early users. The highest-impact wins come when business stakeholders start to feel a difference—when they say, "This helps," or, "This is better than what we had before." That moment matters. Especially because the real impact of data products in terms of business outcomes or time savings often takes months or even years to fully materialize. A quick win in this space doesn't need to show downstream ROI yet. It just needs to make a clear, credible case that value is on the way.

That said, getting to even that first data product can take time. Between aligning business and IT stakeholders, securing approvals, and building foundational pipelines or models, "quick" wins may not feel all that quick. In those cases, it helps to surface and celebrate progress markers along the way. For example, a critical design review is approved, or a business commits to using a product once it is built. Even upstream signals, such as agreement on which domain to focus on, prioritization of a use case, or the launch of a foundational capability like a reference architecture, can serve as wins. These are all leading indicators that the flywheel is starting to turn.

One of the most compelling examples of a quick win I have seen, which unlocked real traction, came from a multinational consumer electronics company. Their global logistics and supply chain teams had long relied on Oracle as their ERP backbone. While core transactions and records remained stable, the company lacked useful analytical visibility into how parts and materials flowed across regions. The tipping point came when the analytics and supply chain teams sat down together to identify which raw, but useful, ERP data could be tapped quickly and routed into their existing cloud-based data lake. Within just a few weeks, they stood up a working dataset covering global shipments, storage handoffs, and transactional routes between manufacturing and distribution centers. Because this came directly from ERP feeds, the data quality was already strong, and minimal transformation was required to make it usable.

The impact was immediate. Logistics planners and supply chain analysts were suddenly able to trace duplicative routing patterns, such as components being shipped inefficiently through multiple intermediate sites before reaching their final destination. They were also able to plug this dataset into existing planning models, making them more accurate and better aligned with operational reality. An unexpected breakthrough came in reverse logistics. By tracking shipments sent out and later returned, the team could begin estimating repair and replacement flows, a dimension they had never been able to measure effectively before. That insight alone started to uncover trends around product reliability, wear rates, and potential design issues. While still early-stage, the internal estimates suggested this foundational win could eventually drive cost improvements of 0.5 to 1% of revenue, a massive contribution to the company's bottom line for something that started as a "quick" win.

3.4.8. Step 7: Sustain Acceleration

With early wins in place, the temptation might be to pause and enjoy the success. But short-term wins should, of course, only be the beginning of a broader transformation. That's why Kotter's seventh step emphasizes the importance of consolidating gains and using them to drive further change. Rather than declaring victory prematurely, this stage is about channeling the credibility, confidence, and momentum earned so far to go deeper and broader. It's the moment to scale successful pilots, expand stakeholder buy-in, and tackle more systemic barriers that may have been too entrenched to address early on.

So what does that mean in a data product context? It means you take the validity and enthusiasm created by those first successful products and immediately channel it into the next arc of progress. You expand, you deepen, you bring in new people, and you start solving the harder problems that were too big or too politically sensitive at the beginning. This is where the initiative begins to feel less like an experiment and more like a movement.

Here are some practical ways to sustain acceleration in a data product journey:

- **Expand the scope into new areas:** Instead of only deepening existing efforts, this usually means creating new data products or moving into new domains, business units, or regions. Early wins give you the credibility to broaden the footprint.

- **Invest in new or improved technical capabilities:** This includes adding more advanced capabilities (lineage, automated quality checks, scalable platforms, and GenAI-enabled consumption) and fixing bottlenecks that slowed the first wave, such as unstable pipelines or refresh cycles that were too slow.

- **Start making targeted business-process changes:** To ensure real impact is felt, begin adjusting the downstream processes where the data product should influence decisions or workflows. Small operational changes can be the difference between "interesting data" and "real value."

- **Strengthen structures and governance models:** With momentum behind you, you can now formalize governance mechanisms such as a data council or cross-functional steering group. These structures help maintain alignment and accelerate decision-making as the initiative grows.

- **Bring additional people and teams into the fold:** Use early credibility to onboard new business partners, analysts, engineers, or product contributors. Momentum increases when more teams want to participate because they've seen evidence that the approach works.

- **Take on more complex or previously avoided problems:** Some opportunities were too political, too cross-functional, or too technically messy to tackle early on. With trust established, you can now revisit these challenges with a far more cooperative environment.

3.4.9. Step 8: Institute Change

Kotter's eighth step is about making the change permanent by embedding it into the organization's culture. It's not enough for people to adopt new behaviors for a few months or for a transformation to appear successful while the project team is actively pushing it. For change to last, the new ways of working must become the expected, natural, default way the organization operates. This often means reinforcing the change through leadership behaviors, hiring and promotion criteria, training programs, performance management systems, and the informal norms that shape how people make day-to-day decisions. Kotter emphasizes that real cultural change only happens after you've demonstrated results consistently over time, where those results help shift beliefs about "how we do things around here." If this step is ignored, organizations tend to slide back to familiar habits, even after substantial effort and investment.

Here are a couple of ways this could apply to data products:

- **Drive data literacy and data culture deliberately:** This is where you reinforce broad expectations, including treating data as an asset, understanding the basics of how data products work, and recognizing shared responsibility for data quality and usage. This is where the real cultural shift happens.

- **Update job descriptions and performance criteria:** What previously lived in project teams or Agile squads now needs to enter the permanent operating model. Role descriptions, performance expectations, and career paths should start to reflect ongoing responsibilities related to data products.

- **Embed data products into governance and business rhythms:** Bring data products into quarterly reviews, planning cycles, KPI discussions, and investment committees. Make them part of how the business plans, measures, and manages itself.

- **Continue to be rigorous about value quantification:** Continue to quantify and track the value being created. Treat this as an ongoing responsibility, not a one-off business case.

- **Integrate ownership and funding into recurring structures:** Move beyond discretionary or one-time sponsor funding. Embed data product ownership, maintenance, and evolution into annual operating plans, departmental budgets, and long-term funding cycles.

Putting the Playbook to Work

This book set out to make one idea practical: data only becomes an asset when it is treated as a product. Something deliberately designed, governed, and cared for with real users and real outcomes in mind.

Along the way, we've broken down what that actually means. We defined what qualifies as a data product and what does not. We explored the core properties that make data usable in practice, such as trust, interoperability, and actionability. We walked through the full data product lifecycle, from identifying the right use cases to planning for retirement. And we looked at what it takes to scale beyond a single team or dataset, through architecture, certification, governance, and change.

There is no single "correct" implementation, no universal tooling choice, and no shortcut that bypasses the need for clear ownership and thoughtful design. What matters is intentionality. Organizations that succeed with data products make a small number of good decisions consistently.

How to Use This Playbook

How you apply what's in this book depends on where you are starting. This book is meant as a playbook, which means you can take different "plays" from it depending on the maturity of your organization, the problems you are facing, and what you are trying to achieve.

For example:

- If data products are still a new concept in your organization, you could start with the kitchen analogies and core definitions. Use them to explain, in simple and relatable terms, what a data product is, how it differs from traditional datasets, and why that difference matters.

- If the understanding is largely there but you haven't started building data products yet, perhaps you can focus on the architectural blueprints and the data product lifecycle. Use these sections to move from idea to execution and to structure how data products are designed, built, and operated.

- If you already have data products but they are not delivering the value you expected, perhaps you can use the sections on data product teams, certification standards, and the maturity framework. These can help you assess how individual data products are performing today, where friction exists, and what needs to change to improve adoption and impact.

More than anything, this book is meant to be used. It is a playbook for real-life situations, meant to help you make concrete decisions, take action, and move forward in environments that are rarely clean or ideal. The frameworks, analogies, and examples are drawn from real organizations and real constraints – they are not abstract theories or idealized models. At the same time, no framework applies perfectly everywhere. Every organization has its own context and realities. The frameworks in this book are, indeed, meant to *frame* how things can *work*. Use them as tools to think, adapt, and move forward in a way that works for you.

Looking Ahead

The importance of data products is increasing. Generative and agentic AI are rapidly transforming how organizations operate, how decisions are made, and how work gets done. But a familiar pattern is re-emerging: the models are impressive, but the real bottleneck is still the data. Ever more, organizations are talking about data readiness and AI readiness, often without a clear way to operationalize either.

Data products are one of the most powerful ways to bridge that gap. Treating data as an asset, with clear ownership, structure, quality, and intent, is what makes advanced analytics and AI scalable rather than experimental. Data products create the conditions under which these technologies can deliver value, safely and consistently.

Have Fun

Finally, indeed, have fun with it.

I've spent well over a decade working in data, analytics, and data governance, and I won't pretend that it's always glamorous. It can be dusty, abstract, and at times painfully slow. Data governance in particular demands discipline, patience, and a long-term mindset if it's going to stick.

That's another reason why data products matter. Almost all data strategy, data management, and data governance efforts suffer from the same problem: it is incredibly hard to connect a lot of thoughtful, disciplined work to clear, measurable business impact. People spend months defining standards, building pipelines, fixing quality issues, or aligning stakeholders, yet the results often feel distant or abstract.

Data products have the potential to change that dynamic. They create a direct line between the work and the outcome. You can see who uses it, how it is used, and what decisions or processes it enables. That connection to real results gives these roles a stronger sense of purpose and elevates them beyond purely technical execution.

If this book helps you have better conversations, make more deliberate choices, or avoid a failed initiative, it has done its job.

Bibliography

Gagliardi, T. (2023). *What Is a Data Retention Policy? Best Practices + Template.* Retrieved 7 19, 2025 from DRATA.com: https://drata.com/blog/data-retention-policy

Geckoboard. (2025, November 30). From https://www.geckoboard.com/dashboard-examples/sales/

Koenders, W. (2022). *My Simple Data Strategy Framework.*

Koenders, W. (2023, July 5). *A simple reference architecture for data products.* From https://medium.com/zs-associates/a-simple-reference-architecture-for-data-products-a2bdc0e7828c

Koenders, W. (2023). *My Simple Data Strategy Framework.*

Koenders, W. (2024). Data maturity models — Why having the capabilities in place isn't enough.

Koenders, W. (2024, October 16). From data to decisions: Engaging stakeholders early for maximum impact.

Kotter International. (2025). *The 8-Step Process for Accelerating Change (eBook).* Kotter International.

Kotter, J. (1995). Leading Change: Why Transformation Efforts Fail. *Harverd Business Review.*

Kotter, J. (1996). *Leading Change.* Boston: Harvard Business School Press.

Salem, S., & Koenders, W. (2023). *Identifying data-driven use cases with a value driver tree.*

Index

www.ingramcontent.com/pod-product-compliance
Lightning Source LLC
Chambersburg PA
CBHW051756200326
41597CB00025B/4571